Apostolate and Ministry

Apostolate an

THE NEW TESTAMENT DOCTRINE OF TH

Karl Heinrich Rengstorf

CONCORDIA PUBLISHING HOUSE

Ministry

OFFICE OF THE MINISTRY

Translator: Paul D. Pahl

SAINT LOUIS LONDON

Concordia Publishing House, Saint Louis, Missouri
Concordia Publishing House Ltd., London, E. C. 1

Library of Congress Catalog Card No. 69-12767

Translated by permission from the original German *Apostolat und Predigtamt,* 2d edition, published by W. Kohlhammer Verlag, Stuttgart, 1954.

MANUFACTURED IN THE UNITED STATES OF AMERICA

Contents

Preface to First Edition

The only purpose of the discussions in this booklet is to make a modest contribution toward the creation of a new and healthy consciousness of office among our clergy. We need such a consciousness today more than has been necessary for a long time. This is the case especially because of the struggles toward which we are now moving and which will decide the internal destiny of our nation. For these struggles there must be at hand a spiritual leadership in our congregations that is sure of its task and experiences joy in its office. Therefore the author believed that he should not wait any longer but publish his views and submit them without delay to his colleagues and brothers in office, even though in somewhat fragmentary form, that they might think them through and, if possible, carry them forward.

Tübingen, January 1934

Preface to Second Edition

This booklet, which has been out of print since 1942 and could not be reprinted at that time, appears once again after almost 20 years because of continuing requests for it. Apart from the correction of some proof errors, the new edition is an unaltered reprint. There are two reasons for this. On the one hand, there was no time for a comprehensive new treatment. On the other hand, such a treatment might well have altered the character of the booklet, the concern of which is independent of the history of the theological discussion on the office in the past and the present, and this perhaps to its detriment.

May it, then, go out once more to meet those for whom it was originally written.

K. H. Rengstorf

Introduction

The question to be treated in this work and to which an answer will be attempted has grown out of an emergency facing many if not most of those who exercise the pastoral office today. It deals with an emergency of which it can actually be said that it is noticeable everywhere, even where it has not been formulated and made the subject of mutual discussion or received literary treatment. If not much more is being said about the emergency than is already the case, the only reason is that it is widely regarded as part and parcel of the office and must therefore also be borne in and with it. Looked at from the outside, the question here concerns a struggle, in many ways quite desperate, on the part of the one in office with the demands his office imposes on him in the administration of the Word of God outwardly and, above all, inwardly. Nevertheless, one grasps the nature of this emergency – especially if he is himself personally involved – only when he disregards the person of the one entrusted with the office. If this is done, the emergency ceases to be the result of a divergence that exists between the person in office on the one hand and the demands of his office, especially those which relate to proclamation, on the other hand. Instead of this it arises from the fact that in the person of the one in office Word and Spirit do not combine in the oneness that is the indispensable presupposition of an unbroken proclamation. If this is correct, the conflict here mentioned is present independently of the person in office but assumes form in his person. But first it is necessary to demonstrate the correctness of this proposition.

We begin by determining the relationship of Word and office. According to Holy Scripture the Word is the immovable foundation of the spiritual office in all its functions. In addition, the Word also determines the form of the office in that it makes the office the office of the ministry. It is therefore also the formative principle of the office. Word and office do not admit of separation from each other without the office ceasing to be office. If the Word comes to naught, the office also ceases; if the proclamation of the Word ends, there can no longer be any talk of an office of the church.

Thus far matters are so self-evident that there is no need of further explanations concerning the relationship of Word and office. Nor are there as yet any difficulties to be noted. These only begin when one passes from the theoretical consideration of the office to its concrete manifestation. Besides the Word as its basis and formative principle, the ecclesiastical office has a second characteristic in the fact that it is always tied to a definite person. As little as the office is conceivable without the Word, so little is it a reality when no one is present to administer it.

Nevertheless, the mere presence of one who holds the office is not sufficient. It belongs to the essence of the Word, the proclamation of which is the task of the office, that the mechanical transmission of the Word in itself does not represent a fulfillment of this task, even if it meets all demands for faithfulness and correctness and also all demands for theological correctness. This is closely connected with the fact that this Word is not a doctrine that comprises a number of practical truths and philosophical teachings reasoned out to their ultimate conclusion, but that it is — or wants to be — a message that comes quite directly from God and which, in being heard, summons man into the immediate presence of God for self-vindication and forgiveness. The character of the Word of the Bible as a divine message makes absurd the merely correct transmission of it, for it could actually be made more easily available by means of writing and printing than through a person in office. That the church did not follow this course and at no time gave up personal proclamation must have been due to special reasons in some way connected with the essence of the Word. One can sum them up by saying that because the Word of the church is not a human doctrine but God's message, it requires a living witness who by his aliveness attests especially the extra-, super-, and also contra-human origin of the Word. As God's Word it cannot do without man's mouth if it wants to get through to man.

At this point the question of the relationship of Word and Spirit to the office begins to be crucial. It now no longer appears as a question of the office in itself but as a question broached with regard to the one in office. It is presented in a twofold manner: from the viewpoint of the Word and from that of the hearer. In both cases the question is at the same time a demand. From the viewpoint of the Word a demand is made and must be made that the one entrusted with the office should himself be able to stand his ground before the Word. Then comes the hearer's question about the right of the one in office to speak and act as he does. It is best formulated by Rudolf Bultmann in this way: "What right has an ordinary man, whom I do not know and who does not know me, to offer me the forgiveness of my sins in God's name simply because he happens to be entrusted with the office of the church's proclamation?" [1]

In this question, as in the demand of the Word, there appears, consciously or unconsciously, the desire that the one who holds the ecclesiastical office should be confirmed by the Spirit in his right to administer the office of the Word. Thereby the Spirit in some form or other is made alongside the Word the constitutive factor of the office. The only remaining question is whether the Spirit enjoys equal rights with the Word as a basis and formative principle, or whether He fulfills a complementary function.

It is significant for the present-day situation that a large number of those in office threaten to go to pieces under the postulate of the Spirit, no matter whether this postulate is experienced as such or not. The Word is present and delivered to the one in office to be administered and proclaimed, but it does not become preaching that flows from inner freedom and is done with joy, because the question as to his right to preach is not settled in the preacher himself – and this in view of the preacher's own defective personality and not in view of the Word.[2] Corresponding reflection is present also in the congregations. Clear evidence of this is found in the state of affairs existing in regard to the confession of sins, which has disappeared but for insignificant remnants.[3] The motives behind this phenomenon cannot be investigated at this point. This must be charged above all to religious individualism, which arose in Pietism, though this does not tell the whole story. Here we shall only indicate quite clearly the danger that threatens the office of the ministry from this direction. An office whose incumbents are not raised above vacillation and who cannot with a good conscience risk publicity with their claim that they have the confidence of their hearers has lost its meaning and right to existence even if God's Word is its basis and determines its form. In practice this is already the case wherever the pastor is nothing but the religious functionary of the congregation, as he has already become long since in wide circles.

In this hopeless situation the demand for the Spirit in no way brings any help, especially not when in practice the demand results in causing the gap between the person of the one in office and the proclamation committed to him to emerge in the clearest possible manner. Only one thing can help the situation along, namely, the knowledge that the New Testament knows nothing of such a counterplay of Word and Spirit in the domain of the office, especially not in the person who has been entrusted with the office, although to him the thought of his personal unworthiness for the office and the seemingly quite accidental manner of being entrusted with the office is at least as familiar as it is to us today (see 1 Cor. 15:8-9). But this poses the question how this firm position of the New Testament toward the office is to be explained and what results emerge from its principles for a basic determination of the essential, constitutive factors of the ecclesiastical office in the strict sense.[4]

PART I

The Apostolic Office in the New Testament

CHAPTER 1

The Apostolate and the Office

At the very beginning of our historical investigation we must be clear concerning the fact that the New Testament reveals nothing that could rightly be compared to the pastoral office of today.[5] The presbyters of the New Testament congregations constitute much less a group entrusted with an office than a position alongside other positions in the congregation [6] – the Jewish example leaves us in no doubt on this score. The bishops appear as somewhat clearly outlined personalities for the first time at a relatively late date, namely, in the Pastoral Epistles. And when Paul in 1 Cor. 12:28 ff. enumerates a number of representatives of the inner and external life of the congregation, he does not mean thereby the incumbents of ecclesiastical offices but people who have received a charismatic gift from God in order that as members of the congregation they might serve the congregation with the gift. How little Paul thinks of offices in our sense can be seen from 1 Cor. 12:31 and 13:1 ff. Here alongside and by the special role of the individual in the building up of the congregation is indicated the service which each member in love owes the congregation and can render to it, and on the basis of which the various powers working in the congregation can develop in a significant manner.

To recognize that the New Testament knows nothing corresponding exactly to our ministerial office does not, of course, fully answer the question whether and to what extent the office of the ministry can be brought into a real relationship with similar phenomena in the first congregation. Only then does it achieve its real justification when the danger has been averted that the answer will fall short when certain analogous features of a most general kind are set forth and the problem itself remains unconsidered. This problem is less often historical than of a fundamental nature; it does not apply to the form or forms of the office but to the consciousness connected with it. The task confronting us is to get to the bottom of the consciousness of office, the magnitude of which the reader of the epistles of Paul senses almost at every step.

The "office" to be investigated here is that of the apostle. This is not the case simply because Paul, the most clearly recognizable figure for us among the early Christians on whom an office had been conferred, was an apostle, but because that which might be described as the New Testament consciousness of office does not become as distinct for us anywhere else as it does in the incumbents of the apostolic office. The opinion that this office is of such a special kind that it is better to take no account of it when one busies himself with the spiritual office in the New Testament alters nothing.[7] The witness for this is no less a person than Paul himself. It is quite true that he assigned a unique role to the apostles in the building up of the church.[8] But this is not to say that he has thereby placed them beside or above the rest of the helpers who participated in the work. In 1 Cor. 12:28 ff. the apostles throughout keep their rank. If they here receive the first place, it is only because their office has the widest sweep and because it goes back directly to Jesus.[9] The congregation by its very nature needs the teacher just as much as the apostle if it wants to stay on the right path, to which the latter has led it.[10] If the teacher wants to render the congregation the necessary service, he must also speak and act by virtue of the same authority with which the apostle speaks and acts. Every possibility of grading is hereby excluded, for both the apostle and the teacher on their part serve the congregation, which is dependent on the service of both of them.[11] Because both have received their "office," no difference exists between them before God.

This knowledge alone makes a correct assessment of the facts possible. The apostle is an "officeholder" among others, but he also has his special and unique task among them, which of itself is also essential for his consciousness. The apostle is the one sent by Jesus Himself to bring the glad tidings, the real exponent not only of the early Christian proclamation but especially of the powers that shaped the beginnings of the church. At the same time he is of all the "officeholders" of the first period the one of whom we have the clearest picture. Hence our method is also justified if we, in determining the substructure of the early Christian consciousness of office, spend some time with him and his consciousness of office, and all the more so because his task is the administration of the Word. Moreover, for us it is here a question concerning the inner undergirding of the office of the ministry in the Christian church of today.[12]

CHAPTER 2

The Name Apostle

The mystery of the firm nature of the apostolic consciousness of office unfolds itself with the analysis of its external expression in the name apostle. It was believed for a long time that this name restricted itself to the confirmation of the mission of its bearer [13] by Jesus irrespective of whether this mission was regarded as historical or not, that is, an allusion was found in it more to the form than to what the presence and appearance on the scene of men like the Twelve and others, including also Paul, really meant in actual fact. Hand in hand with this view went the opinion that in the apostolate, considered in its formal relationship, there was basically a phenomenon of something specifically Christian in the area of Judaism. From here – on the basis of certain discrepancies in the sources – the point was reached where a development in the use of the name apostle in early Christianity was accepted. Even the more extreme view was in part maintained that the name did not go back to Jesus Himself but arose in the early congregation and was only put into the mouth of Jesus subsequently and that this is perhaps how Luke 6:13 is to be understood.[14] But these views are no longer justified since we know that the name apostle does express the actual fact of a mission, but above all a commission and an authorization in the exact measure that the sender himself possesses full authority.

The early Christian apostolate has a previous history on Jewish soil, and this statement admits of no doubt.[15] Here we come upon the שָׁלִיחַ, the ambassador as a fixed entity which in the final analysis bears a juridical character. According to its basic principles it is rooted in the Semitic law pertaining to heralds and appears to be connected with it already in the early parts of the Old Testament historical tradition.[16] It is true that the form שָׁלִיחַ does not actually occur. Only the verb שָׁלַח is found, but the existence of the institution itself is attested with absolute certainty.

The institution of the שָׁלִיחַ, however, received its real expression and ideal establishment at about the beginning of the Christian era in the rabbinate. The basis of the institution is now summed up in the oft-quoted statement: שְׁלוּחוֹ שֶׁל אָדָם כְּמוֹתוֹ, "the ambassador of a man is like the man himself."[17] Accordingly, the ambassador, in everything he says and does in accordance with his commission, to a certain extent embodies the one who sends him. In substantiation of this it may be pointed out that it was possible to become betrothed through such an ambassador.[18] In such a case the latter fulfills all the prescribed ceremonies in place of the bridegroom concerned. That which is enacted thereby is absolutely valid, so that the backing out of the man who is now the bridegroom – not just of the proxy – from the marriage settlement[19] concluded with the parents of the maiden makes formal divorce proceedings necessary.[20] In this case the actual party to the settlement is also free to allow himself to be represented. The authority which he confers on his ambassador is then also very extensive. If, for example, he regrets his decision and sends a second messenger to stay the first one's hands in carrying out his commission, but the latter has in the meantime already carried out the divorce or even merely introduced it, not even he himself is any longer entitled to reverse what has been enacted. The woman who was betrothed to him is now forbidden him forever.[21] This holds in all cases where one makes use of an ambassador of this type.[22]

From the examples quoted it is clear that in the ambassador of later Judaism we are dealing with a legal institution. But this means that only the form is a fixed entity, whereas the content with which it is filled is determined by the particular situation in which it comes into use. Above all, the fact is to be noted that originally the institution had no connection with the religious sphere. On the other hand, the possibility of incorporating this institution into religious contexts always exists. Later Judaism did occasionally make use of this possibility. It is true that the high priest in his mediating role between God and the people was always considered as the one set forth [23] and authorized by the people. In support of the point under consideration Moses, Elijah, Elisha, and Ezekiel are in part described by the rabbis with the honorary title of ambassadors of God, because under His authority they performed miracles which He had reserved for Himself, such as "opening a mother's womb" (Elisha), the providing of water (Moses) or rain (Elijah), raising the dead (Elijah, Elisha, and Ezekiel because of Ezek. 37:1 ff.).[24] As for the rest, precisely this religious use of the concept shows once more in what measure it is determined by juridical and formal considerations and not perhaps by the particular occasion or the particular content of the mission.

If one recognizes this, he is preserved from regarding the Jewish שָׁלִיחַ and the Christian ἀπόστολος as completely different phenomena and also from viewing them on the basis of a formal comparison on the same plane.

Before this can be explained in detail, however, the essential factors that make up the Jewish שָׁלִיחַ must be still further explained and the conclusions yielded thereby must be drawn, namely, that on the basis of a commission limited both in regard to time and essence the ordinary person becomes a שָׁלִיחַ. Basically it is a matter of a single presupposition which the one chosen as a שָׁלִיחַ is required to fulfill if he is to be useful. This presupposition, from the very character of the institution, is of a personal and not material nature. The presupposition is the absolute trustworthiness of the one to be commissioned or the one already commissioned. It is indispensable because with the conferring of the commission the possibility of sabotage is also placed into his hands. The one who has been commissioned with the vicarious transaction of some business can carry it out in his own interests, ignoring his commission, and the one who confers the commission cannot hinder him or annul the commission after it has been completed.[25] But the matter is not settled by the presence of trustworthiness alone. Rather, over and above this there is need of a deliberate, willing commitment on the part of the ambassador to his sender. The whole nature of the institution makes it impossible for the ambassador to discharge his commission in a merely mechanical manner. Just as a large measure of trust has been accorded him, so from him is also demanded a correspondingly high measure of responsibility in the matter entrusted to him. In many cases it is actually his business how he carries out his commission in detail, for the only consideration is that the goal be reached in such a way that the greatest profit is brought to the one who confers the commission. Thus the assumption of such a commission receives the character of a deliberate decision for the plan and will of another. If this is not combined with the assumption, the commission, in the final analysis, loses its meaning; whereas, conversely, the whole life of the ambassador can suddenly experience a radical transformation through the commission that has fallen to his lot, no matter whether it be for a moment or for years. How seriously the rabbis regarded this aspect of the institution is shown by the fact that on occasion it can be said that God is well pleased with an ambassador who risks his life for His cause.[26]

CHAPTER 3

Essence of the Apostolate and Apostolic Consciousness

In every instance where mention has been made of an ambassador above, it would have been possible with equal right to have said "apostle." This is not a theory that could be supported only by the external synonymity of שָׁלִיחַ and ἀπόστολος. The proof for this is supplied by the New Testament of the Syrian Church in which ἀπόστολος is translated by שְׁלִיחָא in connection with the report of Jerome,[27] according to which Jewish men who were officially sent out by their authorities in the manner of Christian apostles with definite commissions were called "Slias," which is nothing else but the Latinized שְׁלִיחָא.[28] And it must be granted that those who translated the New Testament into Syriac knew what they were doing when they chose this word for ἀπόστολος.

For our understanding of the New Testament apostolate and the consciousness of the apostolic office and calling, the equating of ἀπόστολος with שָׁלִיחַ/שְׁלִיחָא is of the highest significance. At one stroke the peculiar nature of this calling becomes recognizable. It also becomes clear why Jesus imparted definite instructions for the conduct of the apostles and why He did not hesitate to allude to important consequences which His commission could have not only for their outward and inner life and possibly even for the continuance of their life, but also must and would have.[29] It also becomes clear why He did not enter into other matters, as, for example, the eventual reward for their commitment and their sacrifice; why, moreover, He did not also hold out to them the prospect of God's miraculous deliverance from dangers to strengthen their courage.[30] The basis for the New Testament apostolate in the totality of its phenomena is the rabbinic statement that the apostle [31] of a man is like the man himself.

The consequences arising from this, if Jesus is put in the place of the sender, describe the duties and rights of the one sent out by Him and also outline every detail of the life he must lead as the representative of such a commissioner. They further reveal how intensely one who has been called as an apostle of Jesus is conscious of his commission if he is a true apostle of Jesus: as an apostle he lives by Jesus' own authority and is conscious of the meaning of this fact. And, finally, they also mark the limits which are set up for such a consciousness of one's calling through the person of Jesus as the sender and which should guard against slipping into a consciousness of office that crystallizes about one's own person and its importance. These limits are at hand in the cross of Jesus, which testifies to the bearer of the office of the apostolate that the life of his Lord was one of service and devotion and that he should reject every egoistic exploitation of apostolic authority as standing in contradiction to the essence of his commission.

According to its historical presuppositions the apostolate is representation of Jesus. This imposes on the apostle, as he views matters from the perspective of the life and cross of Christ, the duty of being "Jesus-like," if one may use this term. There is a private life for the apostle within the terms of his commission just as little as there is room for such in the case of the שָׁלִיחַ; for him there is only an official life in which the commissioner Himself assumes form. On the other hand, the fact that in the early Christian apostolate it was literally a matter of being a representative of Jesus always places a firm foundation beneath the feet of the apostle as he views matters on the basis of the authority of Jesus whenever he gains the impression that the commission conferred on him is too hard for him. Only he is chosen as an apostle in whom one has the confidence that he is able to fulfil his commission, that he wants to do so, and will do so. Hence the call to be an apostle is not only a serious task but also a special demonstration of trust and a promise. If this is already the case in the ordinary relationships of life, it is especially so when Jesus, who knows the hearts, calls men as His apostles.

No one recognized this as clearly as Paul, to whom it was also granted to grasp in a special manner the essence of the apostolic office. In his office he always saw constant proof of the infinite grace vouchsafed to him. He could therefore use ἀποστολή and χάρις almost synonymously (Rom. 1:5; Gal. 2:9; cf. 1 Cor. 3:10; Rom. 12:3; 15:15), although it was precisely Paul who in a special manner learned to know the troubles connected with the apostolate (cf. 2 Cor. 10–12).[32] For him this usage was quite consistent when he viewed his situation as an apostle from the essence of his own and every apostolic office and pronounced judgment on it in the only proper way, from the viewpoint of the sender, in this case from Jesus, and not from the viewpoint of himself as the one sent. Paul therefore thinks and speaks in truly apostolic manner when in Gal. 2:7 he speaks of being entrusted with the proclamation of the Gospel (ὅτι πεπίστευται τὸ εὐαγγέλιον τῆς ἀκροβυστίας).[33]

Against this background, which has been drawn from the actual establishment of the apostolate, it is now easy to set forth its actual manner of manifestation. In this connection it is no longer necessary to discuss at length the question whether it is scientifically permissible to speak of apostles of Christ in the sense that already during His lifetime He incontestably made men His representatives from the circle of His disciples.[34] A few points suffice. In the first place it must be noted that the apostolate is not an office in our sense of the word but a commission limited both temporally and materially, the single presupposition of which lies in the person of the one entrusted with it in addition to his trustworthiness, his readiness to risk everything for the One who gave him his commission. In the absence of distinctive marks of office conferred thereby, a very strong objection is removed which has time and again been felt in connection with the appointment of apostles by Jesus Himself. In addition to this, the idea that lies at the basis of the apostolate is so common in the environment of Jesus that it caused no surprise when He also made use of it. Only one thing is new, namely, that by connecting the institution with His person the function to which He called His disciples by entrusting them with His apostolate is definitely of a religious nature. But this again lies only in the nature of the matter. If it is the office of Christ to bear witness to God's will, to proclaim the coming of His kingdom, and to bring it about, the task of His apostle can only consist in doing the same and in subordinating everything to this goal of Christ.

The result of this is that in the New Testament the dominant factor in the work of an apostle must lie in *the proclamation of the Word.* This was carried out in the first place by active preliminary participation in the work of Jesus,[35] the proclamation of the nearness of the Kingdom of God, which included the calling of the people to repentance (Matt. 10:7 and parallels; cf. 4:17). Thus the office of Jesus also becomes altogether the office of the representatives called by Him. Yet this does not signify any identity between them and Him. Such a relationship is excluded because Jesus can proclaim the coming of His kingdom in His own person, whereas the apostles bear witness to Him as the One in whom, especially after His exaltation, the promises of Scripture and His own proclamation have been fulfilled before their eyes and before their conscience. Alongside the ἐγὼ δὲ λέγω ὑμῖν of Jesus, in a completely analogous relationship, exists therefore the consciousness on the part of the apostle of his unconditional duty to bear witness. This explains why Paul, who according to his own testimony was no overpowering orator (cf. 1 Cor. 2:4 et passim), can say: ἀνάγκη γάρ μοι ἐπίκειται· οὐαὶ γάρ μοί ἐστιν ἐὰν μὴ εὐαγγελίσωμαι (1 Cor. 9:16). Behind this statement stands the certainty that abandonment of the proclamation and witness, however imperfect they may be, would be tantamount to disobedience toward the commission received and at the same time sabotage of the underlying relationship of trust, and the result would be the end of the apostolate. It is basically the same consciousness that Peter and John express in a different way in Acts 4:20: οὐ δυνάμεθα γὰρ ἡμεῖς ἃ εἴδαμεν καὶ ἠκούσαμεν μὴ λαλεῖν. This οὐ δυνάμεθα shows that the ἀνάγκη of which Paul speaks is not a compulsion to which one submits with sighs and unwillingness but a privilege by which God gives rich content to the life of the apostle and insofar as it is apostolic life, meaning.

But the matter is not settled with the proclamation of the Word, much as it may stand in the foreground. Joined to it most significantly, necessarily, and indispensably in the light of the basis of the apostolate is the acting with authority (Matt. 10:1 and parallels) over sickness and the demons. Alongside the message of the nearness of God's kingdom and the witness of the fulfillment of the promises of Scripture is found, as required by the nature of the matter, the miracle demanded in the case of an apostle, as in the case of Christ Himself. This brings the coming of the new aeon also before the eyes of those who adopt a skeptical position toward the simple proclamation. That this action also has a real place in the circle of the disciple, insofar as he was called to the apostolate, is proved by a passage like Mark 9:38 ff. or Luke 9:49-50,[36] even if one does not want to admit the validity of Mark 6:30 and Luke 9:10 (cf. 10:17). From these passages it is clear that authority to perform miracles was not just an ideal expectation for those who were disciples but a present reality limited, to be sure, up to this time to their circle and going back to the personal authorization by Jesus.[37]

Word and deed in combination also appear as the characteristic mark of the apostolate after it was newly established by the Risen One for the time until His return.[38] That here also we may and must speak of a personal reestablishment of the apostolate in the sense of a שָׁלִיחַ institution by Jesus is proved by the role played by Paul's call to the apostolate through Jesus Himself in producing his apostolic consciousness and in the discussions on the rights included in his apostolate (see, e. g., 1 Cor. 9:1; 15:8-9; Gal. 1:10 ff.). But even if this were different, in actual connection with the historical substance belonging to the name of apostle, both in the circle of the apostles at Jerusalem and in the life of Paul, action in the name of Jesus has its firm place beside the proclamation.[39] This, it is true, has now received a different aspect from the fact that Jesus Himself has now stepped into the center of the proclamation as the Crucified and Risen One. It is important to grasp in what measure value is here placed on personal witnessing;[40] from this it follows that also after the departure of Jesus the apostolic office is still regarded as His office and not as one administered and conferred by the congregation.

Especially instructive in this connection is the battle Paul had to wage against the older apostles because of his claim to be a genuine apostle of Jesus.[41] Just because he did not have any witnesses of his call at his disposal and because, on the other hand, he had not seen the Lord together with other apostles but was called into service long after them (1 Cor. 15:8 ff.), he had to endure being regarded for so long as an ἀπόστολος ἀπ' ἀνθρώπων (see Acts 13:2-3: the sending out of Barnabas and Paul by the congregation at Antioch), or as an ἀπόστολος δι' ἀνθρώπου, but not as an ἀπόστολος διὰ Ἰησοῦ Χριστοῦ. And this was the state of affairs until the χάρις[42] vouchsafed to him could be recognized on the basis of the realities effected thereby and also acknowledged on this basis (see Gal. 1:1; 2:9). It is of decisive importance to note that Paul, when he speaks of these matters, speaks of an ἐνεργεῖν of Christ in him as well as in Peter and every other apostle appointed by Him (Gal. 2:8). This ἐνεργεῖν reaches out far beyond the claim that it is the proclamation of the Word that establishes the apostle as the messenger of Jesus. Here the whole existence of the apostle is taken as the basis on which Christ operates, not however in such a way that the apostle becomes a witness of the living Christ only passively. Rather, as a conscious, active witness he is aware of his continuous and unrestricted activity and in fact preserves it unimpaired.

Since the New Testament apostle in any case is "something"[43] only through Him who stands behind him — but because through Him he becomes what, after all, a man can become through only Him — therefore in his makeup λόγος and δύναμις, proclamation mighty in the Spirit and miraculous action in the "name of Jesus,"[44] belong inseparably together (see 1 Thess. 1:5; 1 Cor. 2:4-5; Rom. 15:18-19[45]). This becomes clearly manifest in Paul[46] because none of the early Christian apostles was compelled to take up the apostolic office in the manner of Paul and therefore compelled to make this the object of his meditation and to develop a pronounced apostolic consciousness of office and of self-consciousness.[47] Paul has thus become for us the man in whom the apostolate of Jesus has found its classic expression.

The picture of the New Testament apostle has not yet been completely drawn and in particular the full access to apostolic consciousness has not yet been laid open with the elaboration of the oneness of being and duty in the personal life of the apostle, a oneness based on the fact that he is a representative of the *Christ.* Neither is the picture completely drawn with the elaboration of the oneness of Word and deed in the apostle's official life, a oneness that has its basis in the fact that in the apostle the Christ makes a man His *representative.*[48] For this *the consideration of two further factors* that determine the essential character of the apostle is still required: possession of the Spirit, or guidance by the Spirit, and participation in suffering.

In the *Spirit* the apostle is made certain of the presence of Jesus, who upholds and supports him and carries on His work through him. Therefore it is also invariably a basic factor in the essential makeup of the early Christian apostolate that the activity of the disciples called to promote the work of Jesus begins in direct connection with the event of Pentecost (Acts 2:14 ff.). What the New Testament calls παρρησία has its basis in being possessed by the Spirit – the conscious, joyous devotion of one's life to his task and for his task, and the opposite both of an inclination to sectarian work on a narrow basis and of an ecstatic losing of self in the divine power.[49] From possession by the Spirit springs apostolic universalism, such as moved Paul (see Rom. 1:13 ff.; 15:23-24; et passim). This is actually never spelled out but always presupposed, and this again is possible because for early Christianity the Spirit is nowhere an entity beside the Christ but always and only His own Spirit.

If that is the case, "in the Spirit" the act of Jesus, which is valid for the whole of mankind, necessarily becomes the root of a universal proclamation as well as of the subordination of the whole apostolic line of conduct under the one goal – to win all for Christ.[50] Again, it belongs to the very essence of the matter and is not only a spirited and effective formulation of a personal wish when Paul concludes his great testimony on Christ's act of universal reconciliation in 2 Cor.

5:19 with the words (5:20): "So we now speak on behalf of Christ, as His ambassadors, as such through whom [51] God [Himself] is appealing; we beseech you in Christ's stead:[52] 'Be reconciled to God.'" Paul could not have spoken in this way if he had not been supported by the certainty of constant guidance by the Spirit of Jesus. But he lives from this certainty, and against this background his apostolic consciousness therefore confronts us in all its magnitude.

We discover here also the ultimate inner basis of this consciousness. In the life of Paul as well as in the life of every genuine apostle of the New Testament there is therefore no rift between being and duty, no proclamation-crippling contradiction between one's own ability and his task, and no shattered or dejected consciousness of office in which the incumbent cannot experience joy in his office because at the time when he made his decision for Christ and assumed His commission he made the ultimate surrender.[53] In the life of the apostle there is room only for one thing, or more correctly, One, Christ Himself, who has formed him in His image. For this very reason, however, the Christ is also literally present in His person and in the apostle brings men to a decision. This again is manifested most clearly in Paul. For him apostasy from Christ does not only mean apostasy also from himself, as it virtually is, but conversely, apostasy from Paul and his proclamation is also tantamount to apostasy from Christ. That also this aspect of the apostolic consciousness [54] has found expression in Paul as it was never attained again,[55] has its basis in the fact that there is no one who gave more for Christ's sake than he did (Phil. 3:1 ff.). And if it applies to anyone, it certainly does to the apostle, that Jesus becomes greater, more visible, and more effectual in the proportion that any man to a greater degree for His sake gives up his own will and the molding of life according to it, however pious such acts may be.

Only from this perspective does the special impress of apostolic universalism become understandable as we observe it in the New Testament apostles and again most clearly in Paul. Out of the ardent desire to bring the Gospel to all, a desire conferred with the apostolic commission, does not develop, let us say, the desire to carry out the evangelization of the world on one's own, or even the thought of being alone responsible for the execution of the task. The apostle did not find that in the existence of a whole number of apostles, who were also quite different in their essential makeup and inclinations, the task set for him was made heavier but rather lighter. In any case, competition among the individual apostles was not of his devising, if it arose within the circle of the apostles at all and was not introduced by specific groups in the congregations. The role which James played, according to Acts 15:6 ff. and Gal. 2:1 ff., in the negotiations concerning the freedom of the Gentile Christians from the Law [56] also sets him forth as a man who was anything but a theological systematician. It exhibits him, on the contrary, as a man who recognized the differing natures of the various apostles as being appropriate to the manifold nature of their task, and with this task in mind he accepted the differences as an enrichment and not as an impoverishment, for there is no other criterion for the genuine apostle.

When full fellowship was established in Jerusalem by means of a handshake between the older apostles on the one side and Paul and Barnabas [57] on the other, and when along with it the work of these two groups among the Gentiles was recognized also on the basis of its theological principles and purified from every suspicion of incorrectness and incipient church division, this did not take place so that eventual peace might be established. It was done simply from the knowledge that the apostle of Jesus Christ, like every other representative, receives his allotted task and does not choose it for himself. Hence, when Paul becomes the ἀπόστολος of the ἔθνη and Peter on the other hand the ἀπόστολος of the περιτομή (Gal. 2:9),[58] this hardly signifies subjection of the apostolate under a human system, and still less the waiving on the part of Paul or Peter of the universal claim of their proclamation. The fact that Paul subsequently, as he had done previously, still sought encounter with the Jews and that Peter did not avoid Paul's field of activity[59] speaks against such an opinion. One can therefore say categorically that the "division of labor" in Jerusalem was a clear demonstration of apostolic universalism inasmuch as it is acknowledged thereby that Christ's universal goal excludes every kind of systematizing and that the apostle realizes his true purpose when he is conscious of being an ambassador in everything and conducts himself as such (see John 13:16). This is the case also when it is his ardent desire in his office as representative to "please" Him who gave him his commission and regarded him worthy of His trust in the office. (Gal. 1:10; cf. 1 Cor. 4:2 et passim)

The infinitely high consciousness of the apostle, when he incorporates Christ and so participates in the work of God Himself in Jesus,[60] experiences less of a correction than its ultimate deepening in *participation on the part of the one called as an apostle in the sufferings of the Lord whom he is serving.* At the very moment when an apostolate of Jesus is established, the apostle is inseparably linked with the obligation to suffer and with the fact of suffering. The words of Matt. 10:17 ff. contain much more than the mere establishing of an experience of the early congregation. If they were that, Matthew would hardly have included them in the address delivered at the commissioning of the apostles. But they stand in the place where the subject of discussion is the essence of the apostolic office, and therefore they contain, even if one holds the view that the words were not spoken by Jesus,[61] a profound glimpse into its very essence. Because Christ suffers, His apostle also suffers. That cannot be otherwise. And even if it were otherwise, there would be no conclusive proof in this that the one in question is not called to an apostolate in the full sense, but certainly a painful indication of how much there is still lacking in him if he is to be an apostle of Christ in such a way that he can be recognized as one. This is why it is stated in Acts 5:41 of the apostles, who had just received severe corporal punishment, that "they left the presence of the council, rejoicing that they were counted worthy to suffer dishonor for the name." Not their rescue but the lashes of the scourge are their sign of being genuine apostles of Jesus.[62] The same is true in the case of Stephen [63] when, in the session in which his fate was decided and in the presence of the hatred of his opponents, "his face was like the face of an angel" to them. (Acts 6:15)

Paul must again be especially mentioned. Two references will suffice from the many that could be given. First, attention must be drawn to the whole context of 2 Cor. 10–12. It corresponds fully with the basic idea of the apostolate of Jesus when Paul wins his reputation as an apostle not by special performances or unique personal experiences but by the fact that in his office he had to suffer beyond all measure for the Christ. It is his happy experience that through him Christ becomes greater the smaller and lowlier Paul is in himself and the less he looks to himself. Precisely for this reason his intense consciousness of office is at every moment a humble stooping to Christ. But this does not mean any curtailment of the claim with which Paul makes his appearance as an apostle of Jesus. For those to whom he comes, the only matter of importance is that he administers the unsurpassable treasure of the knowledge of the δόξα of God in the face of the Christ (2 Cor. 4:6). That this takes place in an earthen vessel (2 Cor. 4:7) is true of and by itself, but before God it does not excuse the one who believes that he must despise the treasure because of the vessel. The apostolic office is set forth in Phil. 3:10 ff. even more sharply than here under the thought of suffering, or more correctly, under the idea of participation in the suffering and death of Jesus. At the beginning of the chapter Paul opposes men who appear on the scene with high personal pretensions and threaten to overthrow his work. He does this with a sharp and clear word concerning the way that led him to his present office and goal. In contrast with these men, not he himself but Christ is his one concern. He always wants to become more Christlike. Therefore death in office and for the sake of his office is the ultimate confirmation of his office as an apostle. He now looks forward to death, and it is the object of his expectation and longing.[64] But this does not lead to a paralysis of his powers or to quietism but to the highest activity within the framework of his life's work. (Vv. 13-14)

With this the essence of the consciousness of the apostolic calling and office is to some extent unfolded. It is based on the certainty of being apprehended by Christ as well as of representing Him in His own person and on the fact that He has taken the whole life of the one on whom the office has been conferred into His hands. This postulates an attitude of which the distinguishing feature outwardly is an indefeasible claim on the ear and obedience of all men and of which the characteristic feature inwardly is the deepest devotion to Christ. A vital point is that this claim, in clear recognition of the state of affairs, always remains a religious claim. And it is never the case — and here a reference to Paul suffices — that the honor which is the apostle's due as the representative of the Christ is demanded by him as a man (see the Epistle to the Galatians and 2 Cor. 10:12-13). Thus an adequate barrier is set up both against the self-consciousness of the Jewish incumbent of an office and the Jewish-Christian pseudo-apostle

(2 Cor. 11:12 ff.)[65] as well as against a self-sufficient *imitatio Christi.* The picture that emerges must not of course be schematically split up into an inner and outer side. The main feature of apostolic consciousness of office and – it may be said – of the early Christian consciousness of office in particular is that all marks of cleavage are missing. This is the case because the joyous surrender of life to Christ and the joyous employment of one's life for Christ coincide. And it is through this that the παρρησία arises, which enabled the early Christian apostles and missionaries to prepare for Christ a triumphal progress throughout the whole world.[66]

PART II

The Apostolate and the Office of the Ministry

CHAPTER 4

The Decisive Character of the Office

If one attempts to find the way to the office of the ministry of the church of today by making this view of the apostolate and the apostolic consciousness his point of departure, to determine its essence in the light of it, and to establish its claims by it, he is immediately confronted with a difficulty that appears to be insurmountable and hence seems to require nipping in the bud every attempt of this kind. It is the difficulty that arises from the vast difference that is bound to become obvious even from a superficial comparison of the apostolate and the office of the ministry of today.

Two prominent differences may be singled out. One concerns the way of the incumbent to his office then and now; the other concerns the method of receiving office then and now. If the apostle's and the present-day pastor's ways to office are placed side by side, we have on the one side men taken by Jesus from their former life and led to a completely new way – the way of representing Him – with which they had not reckoned up till now even in their wildest dreams and would have been incapable of reckoning. Paul, the greatest among them, actually became a witness and representative of Christ and His cause in a mighty upheaval from a fanatical persecutor (Gal. 1:13, 23; Phil. 3:6; 1 Cor. 15:9). On the other side stand men who have prepared themselves in a carefully prescribed way to be entrusted one day with an office that has been in existence for many centuries and is carefully regulated – men who have actually attained this goal. If the contrast here is already almost insurmountable, this is the case even more so when one observes the method of receiving office: the former case involved men who were called by Jesus into His service in a personal encounter [67] and equipped with His own authority, the latter case men who had the pastoral office conferred on them within the framework of a procedure of a juridical and liturgical nature (examination, contractual responsibility, ordination) by an ecclesiastical authority.

In our context it is quite sufficient to set off these two related entities and to consider the contrasts between the apostolate and the office of the ministry given with them. At the very least it may then be possible to become seriously aware of the question whether there is an organic union between them and whether it is proper to speak of any real association between them. At this stage it must be asked whether, in the face of such a complete difference, it is possible at the outset to make the apostolic consciousness of office and self-consciousness as they were developed – the apostolic consciousness and self-consciousness of a Paul, for example – fruitful beyond the circle of the apostles, or even to make them a basis for the consciousness of office in the bearer of the office of the ministry today in regard to himself and his office. Does it not much more accord with the facts if one refuses to entertain the blurring of differences and rests content with the recognition of the great differences? And must we not also recognize that the presuppositions for overcoming the rift between willing and being – recognition of this rift lies as an oppressive burden upon the life of many pastors – were given to the apostle through his encounter with Jesus and by being filled by Jesus with His authority, but that in our case today they are lacking and must be lacking in the very nature of the case? Concerning the apostolate, do we not have in the manner in which it is received and in the person of its Author two important points separating the apostolate and the office of the ministry in such an essential manner that there can be no talk of overcoming the discrepancies between person and office in the life of today's incumbent by starting from the apostolate? In the prevailing state of affairs, how can a pastor today be what the apostles of Jesus were according to His will if our analysis of the name apostle is correct, namely, that they were representatives of Jesus whom He himself had appointed and who therefore participated in the carrying out of His own office?

This whole question appears to bring the discussion of the relationship of the apostolate and the office of the ministry to an end in the sense that one does not get beyond negative conclusions. It only appears to do so, but does not in reality. For it does not make the basis of the apostolate in its totality the starting point for setting up relationships of a basic and essential nature between the apostolate and the office of the ministry. The question does lift out certain points of importance which are indeed present and indispensable but still not so conclusive that one would be compelled to make his judgment dependent on them alone. The personal encounter with Jesus is not at all identical with the call to the apostolate. Nowhere near all who came into contact with Jesus became His apostles, not even all who came under His influence in a special manner. Paul's Easter history knows of the appearance of the Risen One to more than 500 brethren (1 Cor. 15:6). But by no means all of them or even the greater part of them became apostles thereby.[68] In the context they are represented as a quite special group over against the ἀπόστολοι πάντες, who likewise had a common appearance of Jesus (1 Cor. 15:7).[69] This fact spells out a warning against isolating and overvaluating the personal factor in the call to be an apostle in such a way that the difference in time between then and today is used to deny every essential relationship between the apostolate and the office of the ministry. The decisive factor in the call to the apostolate is not merely a mechanical seeing of Jesus face to face but being entrusted by Him with the representation of Himself.

It is still possible meanwhile to reach substantially beyond this statement, which already takes in quite a wide sweep, and to do this on the basis of what Paul says about his call to the apostolate. We will never be able to give a rational explanation of what Paul experienced near Damascus, important as that would be for us, already for the reason that he regarded this hour as the decisive hour of his life (see Gal. 1:12 ff.). Paul himself, at all events, was convinced of having seen the Risen One, and in this he found something that was indispensable for himself and for his apostolic consciousness in particular (1 Cor. 9:1; cf. 1 Cor. 15:8). Significantly, however, in Gal. 1:12 ff. the ἀποκάλυψις which he received near Damascus is not delineated and compared with the revelations and appearances vouchsafed to the other apostles, but the commission imparted to him in it [70] and the attitude in which he acceded to it are made the climax of the description.[71] From this it follows that Paul on the one hand could not well disclaim his call as an apostle through Jesus Christ Himself and that he had no wish to do so already for the reason that his fellow apostles based their apostolic claim on such a call. The decisive feature in the Damascus experience for him was his complete and unreserved yes to Jesus' commission to him, coupled with the readiness to draw all the conclusions included in the acceptance of the apostolic office of Jesus.

That this is correct is proved by the emphasis with which the apostle in this passage stresses that his earliest conduct as an apostle contradicted everything that one would in the first instance have expected from him. He did not at once seek the fellowship of the other apostles, but went to "Arabia," where there were neither apostles nor many other Christians. But he went there because the word of Jesus had directed him to the Gentiles, because it had thus called him quite directly into the work but did not in the first instance suggest to him to seek recognition of his new office from his associates and predecessors in office. Without this course of action Paul's encounter with Jesus near Damascus would never have become "the Damascus experience of Paul" destined to achieve significance of such immense proportions in the history of the church. Without this course of action his universal claim to the Gentiles would never have found freedom from that rhetorical moment, the freedom in which he stands before us.[72] This yes of the apostle remains also when the attempt is made to explain in some psychological manner [73] what he himself describes as a seeing of the Risen One (1 Cor. 9:1: ἑόρακα; 1 Cor. 15:8: ὤφθη κἀμοί). And with this the apostolic claim of Paul retains its validity because an apostolic claim always has to be substantiated in life, as is the case with Paul. As for the rest, we therefore stand without question on the ground which our analysis of the name apostle yielded, namely, that Jesus gains a representative form in the man in whose case the yes to his own existence is rooted solely in the full yes to the universal claim of Jesus.[74]

On the basis of the apostolate, the way is thus barricaded against those who would like to make a real separation between the pastor's office and the apostolate because the former is not transmitted like the latter through Jesus Himself. But the erection of such a wall of separation is not justified on the basis of the pastoral office. The grounds for this lie in the fact that just as little as in the time of the apostles does the office today come into the hands of men who have no real interest in it. Already in the manner in which one enters the office of the church – by way of compulsory study and examinations and possibly also through the requirement of applying for a special position – it comes to pass that only such men obtain the office of the pastor who have viewed it as their goal and have prepared themselves inwardly and outwardly to enter it, or at least should have thus prepared themselves. Even though such a preparation, especially an inner one, is often enough missing, the fault for this does not lie in the office and its nature in our time but in the incumbent who has not "discerned" in this instance (cf. 1 Cor. 11:29). When he desires the office, he is confronted with the question whether he wants to have it as it is at hand as the office of the church, as the office whose single task consists in testifying to men of God's reconciling act in Christ and leading them to the point where they live for Christ on the basis of this act, and hence conduct their lives in the consciousness that it no longer belongs to them but to Him (see in addition to 2 Cor. 5:14 ff. and 20-21, especially Rom. 14:7 ff.).

The office of the ministry in our day is inseparable from the apostolate in this central setting of the task of the ministry, and this indeed on the basis of what Christ says and what He established as the content of the apostolic office ordained by Him. Where this basis is forsaken, the office ceases to be what it is and always was according to its essence. The impoverishment of the office and its deformation into a calling beside other callings or into an institution that exists on account of the more or less pronounced needs of the congregation, which in every case are not of a religious but frequently of a social or purely traditional nature,[75] is again not the fault of the office but of the incumbent. Representation of Jesus is possible only when the one called by Him into office goes the way Jesus shows him, not the way that seems good and right to himself. Only where such surrender of the will and life to Jesus takes place on the part of the one on whom the office has been conferred is the basic presupposition provided for supplying him with apostolic authority even today, as was the case in the time of the apostles. This is not the case because of the ecclesiastical apparatus that cooperates in the transmission of the office, but certainly under such cooperation on the part of the ecclesiastical authority. Jesus Christ and not simply the ecclesiastical authority is still the Lord of the office today; He it is who in the last instance imparts it, at least where an office exists in His sense. And precisely for this reason there is still representation of Jesus in the office of the church, representation with His full authority.

But before we go into this more closely and especially before we attempt to ascertain what the representation of Jesus with His authority includes, we shall briefly summarize what has been said up to this point. We saw earlier that the essence of apostolic consciousness is rooted in the conscious decision of the one called to be in his commission an apostle of the will of his commissioner and that it finds expression in the absolute surrender of his whole being to his commission. Here the inner consistency of the apostolic claim has its real basis, and thereby also the success of the early Christian apostle is to be explained. In Paul the Galatians heard Jesus Himself speaking to them, and that without his assurance, but later they had to allow themselves to be told that apostasy from Paul is apostasy from Jesus Christ (Gal. 4:14; cf. 5:4; 1:6).[76] But here we have not only the problem of the apostolic office but also that of the office of the ministry. The question is whether the one on whom the office has been conferred is today prepared to risk making the decision that the apostle made and is consciously and joyfully a witness of the living Christ, and that daily and hourly and in everything. Unity between the proclamation and the way of life in the person of the bearer of a message that not only claims intellectual assent on the part of the hearer but a complete penetration and transformation of his life is the indispensable presupposition for the proclamation to be taken in all earnestness. The Christian message was such from the beginning and is still today. The problem of the ecclesiastical office is therefore in the last instance the problem of the one who has the office, namely, the question whether he is prepared to say yes to such an administration of office and to allow himself to be prepared for it by God.

Thus the essential relationship between the apostolate and the office of the ministry in our church has been established on the basis of the foundation of the office. The relationship is provided in the need for coming to a decision that must be made by those who belong to the generation of preachers and pastors in our day in the same way in which it was made by Paul and will have to be made by the preachers and pastors of Jesus of all time. This raises the question whether they are prepared above all to allow Jesus, His will, and His reality to have full and sole authority with them.[77] Only when this question is answered in the affirmative is the presupposition provided for the presence of Jesus in the one on whom the office has been conferred. Only from the union of one's will with the will of Jesus can the miracle arise that Jesus Himself is speaking in the word of some man and that Jesus Himself is acting when he is acting. Or, in other words, only he who has the courage and will of an apostle, and especially of a Paul, to be Jesus' representative and one who is not just trifling will also be identified as His apostle; only he who confesses Jesus as the Lord of his office is acknowledged also by Him as commissioned by Him (see also Matt. 10:19-20; Luke 12:11-12).

CHAPTER 5

The Lord of the Office

Naturally, the question arises at once how one can attain such courage and will at all. Does not the statement that one must actually run the risk of being a representative of Jesus and not only appear to be one contain a postulate that arises from a basically visionary attitude? Is not reality here left out of consideration in an irresponsible manner and an ideal office constructed that is impossible to find in actual fact and with men being what they are? All this would be correct except for one thing, and if this one thing did not absolutely gainsay such questions and establish in the one on whom the office has been conferred the courage and will actually to be a representative of Jesus. The point here is that Jesus Christ Himself is the Lord of the office of the ministry as He was the Lord of the office of Paul and the other apostles.

If we make the statement that in Jesus Christ the Lord of the office has remained the same since the days of the apostles, many a one will be inclined to regard this as a self-evident truth. This, however, does not alter the fact that it only seems to contain a self-evident truth, for that which lies contained in it is comprehended by very few. The blame for this is not solely but nevertheless in a far-reaching degree attributable to the circumstance that the transmission of the office today no longer takes place through Jesus Himself but through an ecclesiastical authority. Again and again this is felt as a heavy burden among the bearers of the office themselves as well as in many congregational circles that are spiritually alive, because in this way the office can be given also to those who are unworthy. Furthermore, because the incorporation of the incumbent into an official organization necessarily goes with the transmission of the office, this is frequently felt to be something restrictive. Hence enthusiasts of a more or less pronounced type have also time and again taken serious offense at the influential participation of ecclesiastical authorities in the conferring of the spiritual office. And on the basis of the principle that the authorization to administer Word and Sacrament, and especially to forgive sins, can never be a matter for any ecclesiastical authority, they have demanded the abandonment of the method followed hitherto. At any rate up till now they have not given a clear answer to the question by what measures and through which authorities the office should be awarded in their opinion. They would have to indicate in what way they would recognize that one who comes forward with a claim to divine authorization also in actual fact possesses authority from God and is not only arrogating it to himself. Even pronounced spiritual success has never been an infallible mark for establishing the right of such a claim, as has been demonstrated repeatedly in the history of the church. To a man with the clear-sightedness of Paul belonged with good reason the ability to distinguish the false spirit and its claim from the right Spirit and His appearance on the scene in the fullness of His authority, namely, that the ability of διακρίσεις τῶν πνευμάτων belongs to the gifts which God's own Spirit alone can impart to man because man is not capable of acquiring them himself (1 Cor. 12:10). Should that which was a charism for Paul today be at the disposal of every genuine Christian who is concerned about preserving in its purity the office of the proclamation and the forgiveness of sins?

But quite irrespective of this, the reproach that it is not the business of an authority to transfer the office does not hit the authority at all where it is intended to hit, just as little as it hits the ecclesiastical office of one who is *rite vocatus* on the ground that an ecclesiastical authority played a decisive role when he took over the office and that the Spirit did not act alone. Not a single ecclesiastical authority arrogates the right on the strength of a special gift of perception characteristically his own or with complete arbitrariness to choose some individual out of the number of church members as suitable for office and to transfer to him the office of the ministry on the strength of the power at his disposal. The function of the ecclesiastical authority in the transferring of the office is to take care that it is carried out in orderly manner in the name of Jesus and within the framework of His congregation, so that it does not become the private affair of every individual to take up office whenever it pleases him and to give it up again if he has lost his liking for it, or if the original enthusiasm has yielded all too soon to disillusionment. It is necessary here once again to keep it clearly in mind that in general only those receive the office through the authority who present themselves for office before it. Hence the initiative does not lie on the side of the authority, neither on the side of him who is authorized by the authority to transfer the office; it lies solely with those who approach the authority with the wish to be admitted to the administration of the office of the ministry.

Hence the authority is only the hand that arranges matters. Its participation in calling to office does not contradict the statement that also today Jesus Christ Himself is still the Lord of the office. Quite the contrary, in the manner in which it cooperates in calling to office, the authority itself draws emphatic attention to this basis of the office. For this very reason the authority lays upon the heart and conscience of the beginning pastor the permanent obligation of rendering an account of the administration of his office also to it. But he is also obliged to do this especially to the Lord Jesus Christ as the Lord of the church and of the office. This applies especially to those spheres of the office and life of the incumbent which no human superior may review and which are quite beyond the reach of any decree of an authority to set in order from above or from outside. For this reason the real decisions of office must be made time and again before Him and not before the forum of an ecclesiastical authority. This also *takes place* where the Lord of the office is always a present reality for its incumbent. A different attitude is quite impossible if the office is not to lose its character as an office and a commission. A very direct responsibility on the part of the incumbent toward the Lord of the church and the office is imposed by this characteristic. One can speak without hesitation of the pastor's special responsibility to the members of his congregation, not because he stands closer to Jesus than they do but only because his solicitude for them has been made by himself the content of his life. The Lord of the office has not conferred on the incumbent a special degree of honor within the church and congregation, honor that would assign him a special place and allow him to claim special respect. From Him he only receives a special burden in his commission. Insofar as he has a degree of honor, it comes to him from this burden, for in it he is bearing Jesus' own burden, or, better still, in this burden he participates in the office of Jesus, leading men under the sovereignty of God and helping them remain under it. And so the honor of the office of the ministry lies in the service to which its incumbent is called; but this is the case because the Lord of the office Himself saw the meaning of His life in service. (Matt. 20:28)

With these last sentences we again stand in the midst of the apostolic consciousness as we have unfolded it. They apply just as precisely to Paul, whom concern for the fulfillment of his commission would not allow to rest and who found his καύχησις in his sufferings as an apostle (cf. 2 Cor.

11:10), as they apply to the bearer of the office today. The decisive factor, however, is that they immediately link up with Jesus' consciousness of His own office. But this cannot be a mere design. If it were a design, the consciousness of immediate responsibility toward Jesus as the Lord of the office, which moved Paul,[78] and also his consciousness of having been blessed and honored [79] in being entrusted with office by Him, would have disappeared. This would have been the case at least in the course of the centuries, if not already with the apostles themselves, or it would have taken on a new form with the bearer of the office himself and no longer the Lord of the office at its center. Since that did not come to pass, a factor becomes effective in the consciousness which is just as fundamental for the office of the church as it was for the apostolate, namely, the knowledge that in both of them Jesus Himself is at work as the Present One, and not only after the one entrusted with the office has taken up his office but entirely on principle, on the basis of the office and its essence.

In this way the office of the ministry ranges itself immediately beside the apostolate. But the two do not stand beside each other because the one who administers the office of the ministry manages to raise himself to an apostolic consciousness, but because at its beginning, just as at the beginning of the apostolate, Jesus stands as the Lord of the office. In any case, with the office of the ministry this is less easily grasped in actual fact than in the case of the apostolate, where the designation of the incumbent as an ἀπόστολος already clearly proves that one cannot take up the office by himself but only receive it.[80] But the office is still possible with Him, and so by virtue of the fact that only Jesus Himself makes it possible from within and continues His work through His representative the office acquires the character of the apostolate itself. Since the office of the church, which testifies of the reconciliation that has been made and the way that has been opened to God, does not and cannot exist as such but is manifested only on the basis of a conscious decision on the part of a man approached by Jesus to accept His will and goal, we think it is best to reduce this to a personal formula: In the bearer of the ecclesiastical office Jesus Christ today provides Himself with a representative among men in the same manner as He did in the apostle at the beginning of the church. He also fits him out for service with the same authority that He possessed and which He conferred on His apostles.

CHAPTER 6

Office and Spirit

If Jesus is the Lord of the office, it is also His business so to equip the called one for his office that he is enabled to carry it out inwardly and outwardly as the office that represents Him. Here we stand at the point at which the belonging together of office and Spirit manifests itself: in the Spirit the one called into office again and again gains the certainty that he possesses his office as the office of Jesus and that he also possesses the power to carry it out as the office of Jesus.

The church of today still has knowledge of the belonging together of Spirit and office just as it has knowledge of Jesus as the Lord of the office. This finds expression in what happens at ordination. Here not only the office is awarded but the Holy Spirit and His guidance is besought for him who receives the office. Here we again have a fact before us from which we can move forward. It offers us a footing all the more certain inasmuch as the custom mentioned is rooted in very ancient tradition. In the final analysis, it is actually of most early Christian origin and has its classical point of contact in the report of the Acts of the Apostles on the sending of Barnabas and Paul into the heathen mission by the congregation at Antioch. (Acts 13:1 ff.)

It is true that what happens today at ordination, when the Spirit is prayed for, cannot in any way be placed directly beside what happened at Antioch. That is a direct result of the different manner in which the Spirit is imparted in the former and latter instances. It is necessary to go into this somewhat more closely and after some observations finally to arrive at the heart of the matter. In the report of the Acts of the Apostles there is no mention of the leaders of the congregation praying for the Spirit for both men with the laying on of hands. This, however, is not due to brevity on the part of the narrator, but is based entirely on the situation of Barnabas and Paul. As baptized Christians they were in possession of the Spirit long since [81] and were not in need of a new endowment with the Spirit. Nor is it the case that the apostolate of Barnabas and Paul should now for the first time come into actual existence through the reception of the Spirit. The context leaves us in no doubt that they were apostles long since, and not only Paul but Barnabas also.[82] Their designation and call to missionary proclamation through the Spirit Himself is simply taken for granted and not established now for the first time (13:2). If the Spirit is manifested at the moment when it is customary to see the conscious transition of early Christianity at a specially noted place to the systematic winning also of non-Jews for Christ, this must have a basis that does not depend on the receipt of the apostolate nor on the receipt of special worthiness to carry out the apostolate but on the special situation in which Paul and Barnabas found themselves. This situation, the decision of a congregation made up of Gentile and Jewish Christians (Acts 11:19 ff; cf. Gal. 2:1 ff.) to do Gentile mission work, was by no means the concern of the apostles only but just as much that of the congregation at Antioch itself. It can be said that the historical significance of the decision consisted in the fact that here for the first time a whole congregation made a decision for the apostolic universalism of Paul and thereby made his apostolic concern its own.

If that is correct the manifestation of the Spirit in the context acquires a profound meaning, and that in a twofold respect. On the one hand, the breakthrough of missionary universalism in Antioch within the church-historical situation is appreciated in all its magnitude inasmuch as it is established that here God's Spirit and the Spirit of Jesus Himself was at work. Neither the congregation nor the narrator to whom we owe Acts 13:1 ff. had any other way of making this universalism understandable. Tension regarding the adding of heathens to the congregations was so great within early Christianity that the most direct intervention of the Spirit had to be recognized.

But even greater and more important in our context is the second point: the light that falls on the apostolate of Barnabas and Paul and on the manner in which they carried it out. From the way in which the connection between Spirit and apostolic work is here spoken of, it is clear that both men, of whom Paul was conscious of being called as the apostle of the ἔϑνη (Rom. 11:13),[83] could wait until their concern became the concern of Christianity and the invitation to the Gentiles to enter the kingdom of God became a part of the work of the whole church. It is probably permissible to claim that Paul never considered separation from Jerusalem, although difficulties of a rather serious nature were placed in the way of his apostolic concern and his apostolic claims. If he did not do that, there is only one explanation for it. It lies in the knowledge that it was not he who was carrying out the office conferred upon him as his office, but that he was conscious of being directed in it as one fully responsible to his Lord. For him, his apostolate was the apostolate of Jesus. This bound him to do only that to which Jesus drove him in his spirit. In accordance with this, Paul did nothing or expected nothing until the Lord of the office gave His representative the necessary scope, as came to pass in Antioch. It lies at the very heart of the essence of the apostolate that the disclosure of working possibilities is solely the concern of Him who calls men as His representatives, just as He also imparts the knowledge of what must be done and in His authority supplies the power to carry it out.

It would now be a fascinating task to follow this unity

of the Spirit's guidance and the apostolate in the life of Paul more precisely, and all the more so because above,[84] where the apostolate and the possession of the Spirit were already discussed, only comments of a purely fundamental nature were made with an eye to apostolic consciousness. On the other hand, the transformation of the life of an apostle through the Spirit was only hinted at. Reference to a few passages suffices, which all have real significance for delineating the work of an apostle in particular and in all of which his guidance through the Spirit becomes manifest: "being hindered" from proclaiming the Word in Asia and Bithynia (Acts 16:6-7); the vision at Troas, in which Paul saw the call of Jesus to proclaim the Gospel in Macedonia (Acts 16:9-10); the decision to visit the congregations in Greece and, connected with this, the journey to Jerusalem ἐν πνεύματι (Acts 19:21; cf. 20:22-23); the glance toward Rome and other parts of the West (Acts 23:11 et passim); the journey to Jerusalem to "the apostolic council" κατὰ ἀποκάλυψιν (Gal. 2:1); and many other passages.[85] These passages demonstrate the matter-of-course way in which Paul permitted himself to be guided in his office by the Spirit. But it is not this of which we now take note in him. The manner in which Philip brought about a meeting with the high official of the queen of Ethiopia (Acts 8:26 ff.) and Peter came to execute his office in the house of the centurion Cornelius at Caesarea (Acts 10:1 ff.) demonstrate that such guidance by the Spirit is definitely apostolic. This does not mean that it was limited to the apostles. In view of the significance and the manifestations of the Spirit in the first Christian congregations, this is quite out of the question. But this does not at all exclude but rather includes the fact that the apostolate and the Spirit belong inseparably together and that the apostolate operates under the full guidance of the Spirit. This was all the more certain because there was a word of Jesus available, which for the time being was the test of the genuineness of the apostolic consciousness and claim to the apostolate and which brought the apostle and the Spirit in a oneness. (Matt. 10:19-20)

If a concept is to be formed as to what meaning the petition for the Spirit includes for the one who receives the office of the church, then it is necessary to recognize the essential connection between the apostolate and the Spirit and to grasp its real significance. The Spirit is the formative principle of the office and gives the apostle inner certainty. The Spirit also frees him from vacillation in matters concerning the external arrangement of his work. The possession of the Spirit and the guidance of the Spirit make of the sinful man called to the apostolate the apostle and representative of Jesus. He does his work in the Spirit of the Lord of his office and therefore also experiences joy in his office come what may. This is the New Testament situation in the face of which the petition for the Spirit in behalf of the one about to begin the administration of the office of the ministry is spoken. It clearly demonstrates the reality of the Spirit for everyone who confronts the New Testament and the witness of the apostles with confidence. It is necessary to believe in the presence and efficacy of the Spirit in order to experience Him. Christianity also believes in the Holy Spirit and confesses this faith in its creed. It confesses Him as present and working in the whole congregation and in its members.

It is all the more disturbing to see how little practical significance is attributed to this petition for the Spirit, although it has a divine promise supporting it. This becomes recognizable especially in casting a glance at the office of the ministry. It is evident that in wide circles, if not in the majority of cases, this office is regarded only as a heavy burden with which one must deal in the best manner possible, especially in the long run. It is just as if the petition for the Holy

Spirit had never been made. This, however, is not the fault of the ecclesiastical authority nor of the pastor commissioned to carry out the ordination. One may expect of the man who has undertaken to induct another into the office of the ministry that for him the prayer for the Spirit for the new brother in office is no empty form, a mere ceremony prescribed by authority, and that this cannot be for him an empty form.

But even if this were so, even if a mere empty form gave satisfaction, the decision as to what is to become of this petition would still lie with him for whom it was spoken. The Holy Spirit, who in the New Testament is the Spirit of Jesus, can be no reality for him, and then the whole passage has no meaning as far as he is concerned; then it is also incomprehensible how this man is going to carry out his office in a church that reckons faith in the Holy Spirit as one of the three basic articles of its faith. Or the Holy Spirit is for him a reality and a power that is actually effective. In this case it would be an instance of singular faintheartedness not to count unconditionally on the power and guidance of Jesus in the administration of one's office on the basis of the promise made by Jesus for every believing prayer and not to place oneself under His care. This would be strange already for the reason that a man cannot prepare his office for himself but must take it over in its entirety whether he wants to or not, and because he therefore faces a tremendous task with little strength and cannot measure up to the task with his own strength. Where the weak man and the office of representing Jesus meet and it becomes his business how he copes with this office, a conflict and a breakdown is bound to ensue. This must also be the result even if the office has been accommodated to the incumbent's capacity of performance, has been made his office, and thereby becomes a caricature of the office of Jesus.

This is the situation, of which mention was made already

in the Introduction, a state of emergency in which a large section of our pastors find themselves in a hopeless struggle.[86] We now know that it arises when one regards the office from his own point of view as the bearer of the office and not from that of the Lord of the office, and when one holds the view that he must bear the burden himself instead of believing that Another has borne the burden long since, understands it, and possesses the ways and means of making it light for His representatives. Ways and means are at hand in the promise of Jesus that His Spirit will support and lead His representatives. And the promise is fulfilled if one trusts this promise and is prepared to allow himself to be guided by the Spirit. It is quite consistent that evangelical work should have been commenced μετὰ παρρησίας (Acts 2:29) by the apostles appointed by the Risen One only after they had come to certainty of the nearness of Jesus in the Spirit and thereby had become assured of freedom. (Acts 2:1 ff.)

But early Christendom did not only have this but also the other experience, that the office becomes a caricature and a burden if one regards it as his own office and follows in office his own way and not that of Jesus and His Spirit. The classic passage is Gal. 2:11 ff. with Paul's judgment on the conduct of Peter in Antioch. It is evident that Peter was not there in a private capacity. That he acted as he did in the capacity of an apostle is what makes his conduct so full of consequences in the eyes of Paul. Paul labeled it hypocrisy and deviation from the way of truth (2:13-14). He also states how this came to pass, namely, because Peter allowed himself to be controlled by his all-too-human considerations and so abandoned his apostolic independence from every human authority (2:12). Finally, because Peter forsook the guidance of the Holy Spirit, he fell and thus caused a breach between his office and life. As soon as the Spirit cannot work, the conflict between being and duty is unavoidable. This is so in the life of every Christian, but especially prominent in the case of those who are commissioned to bear witness to the new reality that is determined by the Spirit of Christ, whether they administer the apostolate or the office of the ministry. One cannot bear witness to the greatness and power of Jesus if he does not supply proof of the lordship of Jesus in himself.

If we look at matters in this way, the consideration of the relationship of office and Spirit in the light of the apostolate again leads us to the realization that the decision as to what becomes of the office is not contained in the office itself and is not held in the hand of the Lord of the office but must be made by the one who receives it. Therefore it also depends on him whether he promotes or hinders the work of Jesus, whether it is a burden to him or grace. He promotes the work of Jesus when through obedient subordination to the guidance of His Spirit he allows Him to work. This, again, is possible only when he entrusts nothing to himself but everything to the Lord of the office; when he has the further confidence in Him that He knew what He was doing when He conferred the office on him in particular; when he likewise has the confidence in Him that in the plenitude of His power He can set up the weakest of men as His representatives. And everyone who assumes the office should be able to muster up such confidence in Him. It is a tremendous act of grace for all who waver that the form of the apostle Paul stands in the clear light of his own testimony at the beginning of a vast succession of officeholders of Jesus. This apostle said of himself that he was not worthy of bearing the name of an apostle and of carrying out the office of an apostle. And yet he had to confess that the grace imparted to him, in which his office was always included, was not in vain (1 Cor. 15:9 ff.). The mystery of this passage is solved when one understands that Paul did not only preach about the Spirit but placed himself and his office under the Spirit, experiencing in Him the presence and the guidance of Jesus Himself.[87]

Everyone who in his office goes the way of Paul has his experience. For the sake of the Spirit of Jesus, who, according to the New Testament, is truly at work in it, the office is the exact opposite of a burden and a hardship, not only because it need not be a burden if one considers it in the light of its essence but because it actually bears the one who receives it. From the viewpoint of the New Testament the office of the ministry is the most precious thing a man can ever desire even though it is natural to do so in trembling joy, for in it men are regarded worthy of collaborating in God's work in Jesus Christ. It is such also for the one entrusted with the office today if he remains fully aware of how God Himself bears his burden of responsibility. For the office brings the message of the merciful and not the unmerciful God. This applies in the highest degree to those who are themselves entrusted with the office. Nothing more is expected of anyone than he can perform with God's help by the use of his strength.

On the basis of the fact that in the office and in the Word the Spirit Himself is at work and in Him again Jesus Himself, the claim to absoluteness on the part of the church's proclamation loses every resemblance of having been raised for the sake of principle. On the basis of the office, which is conducted in His name and through His Spirit and which continues His work, this claim must be raised also in the face of all disappointments because God so wills it. It is not the case that men cannot come to God also by other ways than the one way consisting in the office of the ministry. God does not bind Himself to certain ways and certain offices. And for this reason the office of the ministry does have its assured place in time.[88]

The Holy Spirit draws us human beings when He wills and in His time through the office of the ministry. Therefore one should at all times regard the oral Word highly and hear it. . . . For God has also ordained that no one should or can believe except through the office of the ministry, so that one should hear His Word, for that is the instrument and channel through which God the Holy Spirit moves the heart.[89]

This is the experience of Luther, who was one of the few men to understand the greatness of the office of the ministry and its basic principles. He himself learned by experience that one receives the office of the ministry in the form of a commission whether one wants it in such form or not. Therefore he also often held up God's promises before Him and reminded Him that because of His cause He could not leave him on his own. And he could do this with a good conscience. Luther was actually conscious that a Greater One was struggling in him for His rights and was therefore guiding and leading him. That he did not comprehend the greatness and the ultimate basis of the consciousness of the New Testament apostle with scientific exactitude and so describe it does not alter anything. He felt intuitively [90] what was under consideration – representation of Jesus – and with a clear eye he saw that the situation is basically the same in the office of the ministry.

For that reason Luther had a strong, direct feeling that the incumbent who did not praise his office was not giving the Giver of the office His due, saying:

When Paul commends his calling so highly, he is not arrogantly seeking his own praise, as some people suppose; he is elevating his ministry with a necessary and a holy pride. Thus he says also to the Romans (11:13): "Inasmuch as I am the apostle of the Gentiles, I magnify my ministry." That is to say: "I want men to receive me, not as Paul of Tarsus but as Paul the apostle or ambassador of Jesus Christ." . . . But this style of boasting is necessary. It has to do, not with the glory of Paul or with our glory but with the glory of

God; and by it the sacrifice of praise and thanksgiving is offered up to Him. For by such boasting the name of God is disclosed to the world.[91]

Luther also says in this context:

The king's emissary boasts and glories that he does not come as a private person but as the emissary of the king. Because of this dignity as the king's emissary he is honored and given the position of highest honor, which he would never receive if he were to come as a private person. Therefore let the preacher of the Gospel be sure that his calling is from God. It is perfectly proper that he should follow Paul's example and exalt this calling of his, so that he may gain credence and authority among the people. In the same way the king's emissary elevates his office and calling. To glory this way is not vain but necessary; for he does not glory in himself but in the king who has sent him and whose authority he seeks to have honored and elevated.[92]

That Luther is not guilty of enthusiasm here but speaking "in the Spirit," that is, in accordance with his office, and that his παρρησία is not artificial but of the type of παρρησία of the apostles is shown by another statement of his on Gal. 1:1:

It is not lawful for me to forsake my assigned station as a preacher, to go to another city where I have no call,[93] and to preach there. . . . I have no right to do this even if I hear that false doctrine is being taught and that souls are being seduced and condemned which I could rescue from error and condemnation by my sound doctrine. But I should commit the matter to God, who in His own time will find the opportunity to call ministers lawfully and to give the Word. For He is the Lord of the harvest who will send laborers into His harvest; our task is to pray. (Matt. 9)[94]

Here we have the same attitude that we found to be the basic attitude of the apostle Paul on the strength of Acts 13:1 ff.: being bound by the Spirit to trust and obey the Lord of the office, who does not allow His business to slip out of His hands even though at times it may seem that way, but who in His time reaches His goal, perhaps even through other people. Although Luther does not here speak expressly of the Spirit, this does not in any way militate against this interpretation of his words. In Gal. 2:11 ff. vis-à-vis Peter, Paul again did not appeal to the Spirit and His guidance for his own person. That he carries out his office in the Spirit and through the Spirit is so directly a part of his office as a representative of Christ that any further word on this matter is unnecessary.

So there is only one way to the office of the church as the office of the representation of Jesus: one must reckon with the presence and power of His Spirit and perform his office in the strength of this source. This was Paul's way and Luther's way, and on it they became promoters of His work. Wherever this course is followed, the office not only becomes less oppressive now or at any time – not "easier"; this certainly will not make it easier but rather harder – but also more fruitful for oneself. The moaning over what cannot be attained ceases, and thankful joy over what we are permitted to attain begins. And for this very reason measurements and comparisons cease. It is not our concern but Another's, and He will see to it, but as a merciful Lord who knows whom He is calling into office (see 1 Cor. 3:5 ff., especially 3:14-15). It is a truism, but it must still be stated, that God's Word would find more response among our people if we had more pastors for whom office meant the exact opposite of a professional or an academic position among others, and above all the opposite of a task in the sweat and under the groans of everyday living. This would be the case if their most precious possession and daily joy in life consisted simply in the fact that in this life God Himself by His Spirit makes them, as Jesus' representatives, His co-workers in His work of grace among the human race.

CHAPTER 7

The Office of the Coming One

The apostolate and office of the ministry are linked together by the fact they are the representation of Jesus in His Spirit. This oneness is adequately grasped in its full depth only when one understands that both are to be considered as the representation of Jesus in His Spirit as the office of the Coming One.

In the case of the apostolate this is a given factor without further ado in the situation in which Jesus and His apostles found themselves when, after His resurrection, He called them as His apostles and representatives for the second time and for good.[95] Now their commission was no longer valid only for a limited period of time but for the entire period between Easter and Jesus' return. It makes no difference here that the darkness of divine mystery lies over the length of this period and that even Jesus Himself had nothing to tell His disciples about it (see Acts 1:6-7). But this does not involve any contradiction with the essence of the apostolic office as it was unfolded above. On the contrary, one must say that with respect to the apostolate it could not be different. The responsibility of the apostle is solely the administration of the office committed to him and nothing more. Similarly, he is not to ask what the One who commissions purposes with His commission in the final analysis and what He will do when the commission is carried out.

For the apostles of Jesus this statement had special significance because they were expecting the end of things and Jesus' imminent return to them to set up His sovereignty. Without the certain expectancy of the near approach of the last days the apostolate would never have become what it did become in the history of the church. The consciousness of the apostles concerning the nearness of the end and of the Parousia became alongside the commission of Jesus and inseparable from it the mainspring of apostolic work. "From the eschatological suspense, from the certainty that 'it is the last hour,' missionary activity and desire received their most powerful impulse. The prospect of the immediate end . . . means the highest straining of one's powers."[96] Therefore it was also the goal of Paul's life and work from Jerusalem and the eastern parts of the empire to fill the West with the Gospel of Christ (πεπληρωκέναι τὸ εὐαγγέλιον τοῦ Χριστοῦ, Rom. 15:19; cf. 23-24), and therefore his work also appears as σῶσαι: to save from a danger that is irresistibly moving over the whole of mankind from the judgment of God.[97] (See 1 Cor. 9:22 et passim; Rom. 5:9; 1 Thess. 1:10)

Against the background of the eschatological expectation of the original congregation the magnitude of the working goal of the apostles and especially that of Paul is not only manifested in all its clarity but especially also the manner in which they regarded their office and carried it out. First of all, it is necessary to recall their estimation of everything that they had to accept in the administration of their apostolic commission. As certainly as suffering by the apostles was indispensable for themselves as divine authentication,[98] so certainly it was also nothing that could have become for them a goal in itself. This is excluded by the fact that the apostles were conscious of being representatives of the Christ in the age that had rejected Christ Himself. Since their office was the apostolate of the Christ, their lot had to be apostolic suffering in the nature of Christ's suffering. But as suffering in the nature of Christ's suffering it pointed the apostles beyond this age to the age in which suffering would end with the manifestation of the δόξα of Jesus.

Paul's great statement, ὅτι οὐκ ἄξια τὰ παθήματα τοῦ νῦν καιροῦ πρὸς τὴν μέλλουσαν δόξαν ἀποκαλυφθῆναι εἰς ἡμᾶς (Rom. 8:18; see also 1 Peter 5:1), contains more than simply a piece of primal Christian hope. It is unthinkable without the apostolic situation of the man who spoke it in the νῦν καιρός, and it is characterized by the very fact that it brings παθήματα upon παθήματα on him. Suffering would have been intolerable for the apostles – especially in the long run – if they had not continuously kept their eyes raised above and forward into the future of the κύριος and the age that dawns with His coming. Therefore the apostolate, as we have it in the light of the New Testament, is also unthinkable simply on the basis that the giver of the commission is the Risen One. As indispensable as this certainly was for the apostles, so indispensable for them – if not even more – was the other certainty that the future belonged to the Lord of their office and that the time is coming in which "at the name of Jesus every knee should bow . . . and every tongue confess that Jesus Christ is Lord, to the glory of God the Father." (Phil. 2:10-11)

It is through this certainty that the name apostle first receives its full content and tone. The whole concept of the apostolate includes the thought that a time is coming for the apostle in which he will have fulfilled his office and will return it into the hands of the One who commissioned him with it. We would not have a genuine apostolate in the New Testament if the case here were not as it is wherever apostles and representatives appear. The commissioner does not let His business slip from His hands and sight for a moment, and least of all when He calls apostles. They are there only to collaborate with the full use of their strength in the attainment of the commissioner's goal and in His sense. This is and remains the apostle's goal. And yet it is precisely when the basic correspondence is determined in this way that the infinite difference emerges that separates the apostolate of Jesus from every other apostolate. In all other cases of the apostolate the attainment of the set goal depends on a whole number of factors over which neither the apostle nor his commissioner is lord, and therefore also in all other cases the attainment of the goal is not really certain. On the other hand, in the apostolate of Jesus that which supports the apostle and permits him to be joyful in his commission even in a hopeless situation is the certainty that the Lord of the office reaches His goal just as certainly as He is the Lord of the office. Because the Lord of the office is the Coming One in any case, there is no wavering for His apostle, no despondency, and even to a greater degree no despondent abandonment of His commission.

It is, however, very significant that the certainty that the Lord of the apostolic office is the Lord of the future did not simply lead to a slackening of the momentum of the vigorous activity of the apostles. On the contrary, the New Testament apostolate, in the early Christian expectation of Jesus as the Coming One, in addition to its inner certainty also gains the powerful earnestness that meets us everywhere in its representatives. On the other hand it attests to its genuine character as the apostolate of Jesus and the opposite of an ecclesiastical institution in the fact that over and above the certainty of office, which springs from the expectation of Jesus as the Coming One, the earnestness of office posited therein is not forgotten but has thereby received a magnitude no more to be surpassed. If, on the one hand, it is "worth one's while"—insofar as one may use this term at all—as an apostle of Jesus to risk staking one's life because Jesus is the Coming One, there springs from the certainty of the Coming One, on the other hand, the powerful sense of responsibility that rests on the apostles of Jesus vis-à-vis His coming. If they are His representatives, the day of His return is the day of the attainment of the goal for Him and for them. But for them, in addition, it is the day of accounting on which they must render an account of their administration of office. This commission is universal and applies on the one hand to the whole of mankind (Matt. 28:19-20).[99] On the other hand it applies to those who already acknowledge the Lord of the new age (see John 21:15 ff.).[100] Hence it can be carried out only when nothing more exists for the apostle but his commission, so that even if he does not reach the goal set up for him he is at the least found faithful and falls under the mildest possible judgment. (1 Cor. 4:2 et passim)

In spite of such magnitude of the apostolic consciousness of accountability in the face of the coming judgment, the basis of apostolic consciousness is not fear but thankfulness and joy. Something quite different in fact from what one would expect in the first instance! At any rate, we now know where the reason for this lies. It lies in the fact that the apostle of Jesus can only regard his position as a conferment of grace, which the Coming One allows to be imparted to him inasmuch as He makes him His representative and co-worker in the attainment of His goal.

The apparent paradox that in the consciousness of the apostle the certainty of a tremendous responsibility over against the Lord of the office and the certainty of a tremendous conferment of grace through the Lord of the office stand beside each other without coming into tension solves itself on the basis of the fact that Jesus, the Lord of the office, is the One who is coming again. This sentence is of basic significance. As little as the apostolic office as such would have been possible without the resurrection of Jesus, and as little as the carrying out of it would have been possible without His exaltation and without the sending of the Spirit through the Exalted One, so little could it have raised itself above the level of a human institution with its external and above all inner shackles and bondage if it had not also been the office of the Coming One. It is only as the office of the Coming One that it made of its incumbents men who were independent of the binding ties and opposition of their time and of the present time in particular, men who were also free of themselves. For this very reason they were in a position to speak to a world unfree and in bondage the message of their liberation through Christ and thereby the word of great joy—and this in the last days and the expectation of the coming judgment.

On this plane, then, the apostolate and the office of the ministry meet for a final, decisive encounter, decisive because it yields definitive clarity on the essence of the office of the ministry. Here also the encounter takes place in the person of the bearer of the office. When we consider the administrators of the office of the ministry, we do not just have ordinary men before us but men who have the commission given by Jesus to attend to His business for Him. This commission they receive at a time and in the midst of a humanity with the characteristic that their members are continuously faced by a decision between God and Satan, between Christ and Antichrist, between obedience and enmity toward God. A comprehensive formulation can therefore be confidently drawn up. The situation indicated is by no means only that of those who have not yet found their way into the congregation of Jesus. On the contrary, the decisive character of the present time [101] makes itself felt precisely in those who confess Jesus and "want to be Christians in earnest," and also in those who administer His office.

The necessity for constant decision in the present time already suffices to demonstrate that "this time" stands under the sign of expectation and not under the sign of fulfillment. But even still more can be said, especially with a view to the ministry. If our time and the situation of the individual man in it vis-à-vis God can be understood only from the viewpoint of the future,[102] this concerns the office of the church in high degree. One must be clear on the fact that after the conclusion of this time there will be no more need of a spiritual office. In His coming kingdom Jesus Himself will again conduct His office and then be the one and only ποιμήν and pastor of the one congregation that is named after Him.[103] The office of the ministry is therefore just as transitory as this time. In this respect it differs in no way from the apostolate of Jesus as Paul and the other apostles were obliged to conduct it. According to its essence, it is just as temporary as the office of the apostles and disappears automatically at the moment in which the time of waiting is past and the time of fulfillment dawns. Hence the office of the ministry has this in common with the apostolate, that its work must indeed be done in the present time and also under its hard conditions, but that it derives its meaning and power from the future, which is the future of Jesus.

This statement is of strong significance for the bearer of the ecclesiastical office insofar as it makes him dependent on the future and therein on Him to whom the future belongs. The future of Jesus is indeed conceivable without the office of the ministry, at least from our point of view, but not the office of the ministry without the future of Jesus.

If this is recognized, formulation of the question under which in many cases (especially in the area of Lutheranism) discussions on the spiritual office were conducted about the middle of the last century becomes completely impossible. The controversy centered on the question whether the office preceded the church or the church the office. A. v. Harless adopted with emphasis the principle that "the existence of a believing congregation is a prerequisite for the office and government [of the church], not the office and government a prerequisite for the existence of a believing congregation." [104] The sharpest contradiction was offered by A. F. C. Vilmar.[105]

He defended the thesis that there could be no congregation without the proclamation of the Word of the apostolic office and of the office of the ministry that followed it, for according to his opinion, "the meditation and reading of the Word may convert an individual, but it never gathers a congregation,"[106] that is, the Word gathers a congregation by serving only as a means when it is proclaimed through the office.

F. Delitzsch radically modified the alternative here set up by reference to the first Pentecost. For him "the same act of God by which the congregation . . . received its life in the Spirit . . . set forth the office with its life-giving activity for the congregation out of the congregation, so that the congregation does not precede the office and the office the congregation."[107] That an attempt is actually here being made to overcome the alternative is not altered factually in any way if it is known that these words were directed against circles who wanted to make the office a function of the congregation. The thrust of the statement is to demonstrate that this must not be considered and that the office is under no circumstances a "creation of human election . . . but, like the congregation itself, a divine foundation within itself and for itself."[108] By referring the origin of the office and the congregation to the divine act of the outpouring of the Spirit, the tension, to say nothing of the rivalry, between both is basically set aside and resolved into a significant and necessary existence side by side and with each other, even if it is not actually a "to each other."

If discussion on the relationship of the office to the congregation has nevertheless continued so that it has not been altogether concluded even today, the reason is that F. Delitzsch's approach has not been carried through and the thought he presents has not been developed to its final conclusion. Irrespective of all historical questions posed repeatedly by Acts 2:1 ff., the question to be discussed does not admit of a solution exclusively on the basis of the divine act of the outpouring of the Spirit because, insofar as we can infer anything concerning the matter in question from the reports, the Pentecost event does not signify the beginning of an office but only the beginning of the activity of its bearers.[109] At any rate, they had already waited for the right moment to make a public appearance. According to the reports at hand, no one else but Jesus Himself had supplied the occasion for this through the promise of the Spirit. (See Luke 24:49; Acts 1:4-5; John 15:26-27; et passim)

But how did Jesus come to announce this promise? We would be misunderstanding the words of Jesus which we have on this matter if we found in them nothing but the attempt to comfort the disciples in the face of the imminent separation of Jesus from them and if we understood the sending of the Spirit only from this angle. The Pentecost event would have never won the central significance for the first congregation that it did win if its motive had lain in the situation of the small crowd of Jesus' followers. This would have been the case had the Spirit come only to lead them out of their forlornness. Its central position and its place beside the fact of the empty grave and the appearance of the Risen One the Pentecost event has in the meantime preserved, certainly not by way of human feelings and judgments but, like Easter, only because it was the manifestation of Jesus, that is, as an event that acquires its meaning because Jesus is acting; it was and is indispensable beside the Easter event. This can be formulated briefly and pointedly like this: In the manifestation as the Risen One Jesus offers proof to His own that He is the Living One and thereby also that He is the One whose universal claim is just as valid as the absolute trust His own place in Him. But over and beyond this, in the outpouring of the Spirit He also proves Himself to be the One whose activity has no end in the world and thereby proves that He is the Present One and the Coming One. If Easter justifies the cross of Christ and gives it its final meaning, then Pentecost justifies the existence of an office and a congregation of Jesus and gives them their meaning in His continuing activity that takes place in His own and through them until He comes again and ends His activity.

Only when looked at in this way does the divine act in the Pentecost event gain the constitutive power for office and congregation that F. Delitzsch wanted to attribute to it, although he was not completely successful because he stopped with the historical event and did not dig deeper into the subsoil. If that is done, it can be seen that in actual fact the accent in the Pentecost account is on the action of Jesus as the Coming One in the sending of the Spirit and not on the sending of the Spirit as such. This point is also established in the character of the Pentecost event as the self-attestation of Jesus as the abiding and future Lord of His own, when precisely on this day the leaders of the congregation step out from seclusion into the open with the Word from Him. Furthermore, it is significant that Peter in his address to the people speaks of the cross and resurrection of Jesus and that he can now do this μετὰ παρρησίας (Acts 2:29). The sobriety and self-evident manner in which this takes place proves that something more happened here than that the distracted group of adherents belonging to a rejected prophet suddenly and in an inexplicable manner gained courage openly to confess Him despite everything.

What Luke reports in Acts 2:1 ff. is nothing else but the fact that Jesus is now raising anew through His apostles the claim for which He was crucified and doing so without limitations. On this basis also the interest of the early Christian tradition in the so-called miracle of languages in the Pentecost event [110] finds its explanation: In this event it becomes perceptible that the Gospel and in it Jesus Himself is calling the whole world of nations to a decision whether it will be for Him or against Him. This question is of tremendous importance for everyone because the One who was rejected and crucified is the Lord of the future, and so it is only fitting that what Peter, according to the Acts of the Apostles, said on this day should reach its climax in the call to repentance and in the offer of forgiveness and saving fellowship with the Coming One. (Acts 2:38 ff; cf. v. 34)

These last considerations also show in what way alone the relationship of office and congregation is to be determined on the basis of the New Testament. As little as they depreciate the congregation over against the office – because in the Pentecost event the congregation too was filled with life – so emphatically does it also follow from these considerations that the responsibility for what now happened after Pentecost rested in the first place with the apostles and thereby with those entrusted with the office as representatives of Jesus in the congregation. This was not the case because they now stepped forward with courage and determination but because in them Jesus as the Coming One created representatives of His claim. If this is noted, it is impossible to arrive at a determination of the apostolate and the congregation which attributes primacy to the apostolate. In either case, if primacy were attributed to the congregation, the historical meaning of the apostolate as well as of the congregation would be given up and thereby also their living area. And this means that both have no other aim but to attest in their respective spheres to the primacy of Jesus as the coming Lord.

In the light of what has already been pointed out no proof is required that all this applies also to the office of the ministry in the same way as it applies to the apostolate. Hence we can now also dispense with applying this in a special way to the office of the ministry. Here the observation suffices that it must and will come to the splitting up of the office of the ministry and the congregation if the eschatological character of both is not adequately kept in sight and if the definitely antisecular nature of the office of the ministry is not preserved. Therefore a systematic transfer of the state's principle of leadership to the church and its chief spiritual offices, as well as to the congregational pastorate, would at the very least present the danger of a secularization of the office in the sense of introducing the autonomous factor. In the same way, moreover, on the basis of the New Testament, founding the ecclesiastical office solely on the authority of the congregation is to be rejected most decisively. The office of Jesus, in the sense of the apostolic office of early Christianity, is present only where the office of the ministry is acknowledged to be the office of the Coming One within the confines of His congregation and where men are prepared to administer it in this sense.[111] Because Jesus is the Coming One, he who has the office of a pastor does not have to be a church official or a functionary of an individual congregation unless he makes himself such, and for the same reason there is no hierarchy in the church as far as Jesus is concerned.[112] The one as well as the other is possible only if men press themselves into the presence of the Coming One. But thereby the office ceases to be the office of Jesus, the office of the church, and an office of the New Testament in particular, whether it is the office of the ministry or an episcopal office.

If the office of the ministry is the office of Jesus as the One who is coming again and is accepted as such, its incumbents obtain the same freedom and joy from the administration of their commission as the apostles did, because in their sole dependence on the Lord of their office they are sure, not indeed of their own business but of His business. Such certainty is an unconditional prerequisite of the administration of the commission especially in times like ours. We must not deceive ourselves for a moment that we are facing the heaviest of struggles as far as the decision of our people, or at least large sections of our people, for or against Jesus Christ is concerned. The office of the ministry in our church will be equal to these struggles only when its incumbents learn, like the New Testament apostles, to expect nothing from themselves and for themselves, but everything from the Lord of their office and of the church because He is the Coming One to whom the end will belong. The apostles lived from this certainty, and therefore the Coming One achieved His victory through them.

The comprehension of this fact, however, brings us to the portal of a final insight. In the past years it has often been stated that the church must expect its future servants to be prepared for martyrdom. At the time when this opinion was voiced, Bolshevism with its hatred of all religions stood as the threatening danger before our people and before our church, and it seemed advisable to familiarize oneself with the thought of dying for the Gospel. Understandable as the watchword was, it nevertheless proved to be quite false. It was false because men looked to coming events from the viewpoint of the one entrusted with the office and not from the viewpoint of the Lord of the office. Over and above this, it was also forgotten that the Lord of the office is the Coming One who holds the victory in His hands.

From His viewpoint the thought of dying has meaning only insofar as death in office is also part of His office for the incumbent. Because Jesus is the Coming One – to adopt a variation of a well-known statement of W. Flex concerning the service of a lieutenant in his *Wanderer zwischen beiden Welten* – the whole stress in the office lies on *life* in representing Him, and dying could of course at some time or other form a part of this life in representing Him. The thought of dying must therefore take up its position unconditionally behind that of living. All sentimentality here, be it ever so pious, is of evil because it hinders the activity demanded by the office. Office and life and not office and dying belong by nature together. Since Jesus is the Coming One, it is altogether consistent that the one in office risks his life in the representation of Jesus so completely that no moment is lived in vain if it is really lived in His office, not because a reward could one day be granted him for sacrificing himself but because he is permitted to be the instrument of Jesus in the attainment of His goal (see Luke 17:10).

From the thought that the Lord of the office is the Coming One every semblance that the fulfillment of the commission is bound to a definite result and that what the incumbent achieves on the basis of his own judgment has any relevance is also thus excluded. It is not his business to achieve results and certainly not to regard his work as successful. His only concern is to stake the entire impact of his whole existence and do this with a thankful attitude that is conscious of its responsibility. This can be the incumbent's only answer to the imparting of the office through Him to whom the future also belongs apart from him, but which he will obtain with Him. With such an attitude he necessarily compels those who meet him to come to a decision, because with this attitude the Christ Himself has found form in him. And it is his office, which he has received from the Coming One, to constrain men to a decision wherever his voice reaches. This is to be done not only before the possibility of deciding for Him disappears with His appearance at the dawning of His sovereignty for the coming judgment, but it must be done also before the possibility of coming to a decision for Him and along with it the opportunity of complete fellowship with Him disappears forever.

CHAPTER 8

The Proclamation

With all this the fixed relationship of the ecclesiastical proclamation is given as the one method willed and ordained by God to call men to a decision for or against the Christ and to win them for His kingdom or to separate them from His kingdom. For the one entrusted with the office of representing Jesus another way than the way of witness to the Crucified One, who is the Present and the Coming One, is given just as little as it was given for the apostles.[113] Naturally, this does not mean a depreciation of the life of the one on whom the office has been conferred over against his proclamation. Because the office is of an apostolic nature, the commission includes the shaping of life through the commission. Only he who does not recognize the apostolic basis of the office of the ministry can actually come to regard the life of the incumbent and his proclamation as two factors which could fall apart, although this does not happen. From the viewpoint of the apostolic basis of the office of the ministry, if its incumbent is not ready for complete devotion to the commission, his commission and with it his office as the office of Jesus falls to the ground, and this then removes from his proclamation the character of a commission. Without distorting the picture, it is therefore possible to say that it lies in the essence of the office of Jesus to speak of Him. It can even be said that according to the essence of the office one has already given up the commission assigned with it when proclamation moves into the background in the face of other functions, or when the tendency or the wish exists to allow it to move into the background.

If the proclamation is that feature of the office by which it becomes recognizable as office and commission for him who has received the commission, as well as for those on whose account the commission has been given, all depends on whether or not it is carried out according to the office and hence in agreement with the basis of the office. The proclamation is carried out in accordance with the office when every appearance that it is only the preacher who is speaking is removed and when the attitude of the preacher leaves no doubt that the cause represented by him is his most personal concern. There is no statement of a preacher in the history of the Christian church that gives such clear expression to this as the words Peter and John spoke before the chief council when accused for the sake of the Gospel: οὐ δυνάμεθα γὰρ ἡμεῖς ἃ εἴδαμεν καὶ ἠκούσαμεν μὴ λαλεῖν (Acts 4:20). Here the personal tie of the one on whom the office has been conferred with the content of his commission receives such strong expression that all possibility of isolating him from his proclamation is missing, no matter whether he himself had an interest in such isolating or whether the attempt to silence him was made from without. There is no other way to stifle the apostolic proclamation but to close the apostle's mouth by force. The proclamation of an apostle ends only with his death.

The characteristic feature of the apostolic proclamation, basically considered, is that it is central. It knows but one theme: God's act of salvation in Jesus Christ at the turn of the times. Paul's word to the Corinthians, οὐ γὰρ ἔκρινά τι εἰδέναι ἐν ὑμίν εἰ μὴ 'Ιησοῦν Χριστὸν καὶ τοῦτον ἐσταυρωμένον (1 Cor. 2:2), is the motto all apostolic proclamation of the New Testament. That is the source of the many indicatives characteristic of the New Testament declarations. The crucifixion of Christ and His resurrection are the unshakable facts on which every single word of the apostles and their disciples rests, no matter what the immediate question they are discussing, and alongside them is the sure look into the future of Jesus, who lends tremendous earnestness and tremendous emphasis to every one of these words. For the men who speak here all this is such literal truth that they do not entertain the slightest thought of being obliged to offer proofs for their basic statements before being permitted to interpret the history of humanity and the history of their hearers with the assistance of these statements.

This claim of the apostles for the absolute nature of their proclamation – that a crucified one is the Messiah and the Son of God and that He is the Risen One and the Coming One – naturally becomes a σκάνδαλον and μωρία for those who confront Him only with rational considerations and without πίστις (1 Cor. 1:18 ff.). It is meanwhile significant that the bearers of the apostolic proclamation did not discern in this an attack on the honor of the messengers of Christ but rather a confirmation of their authority also through their opponents. Paul in particular felt that the rejection of his message in the manner mentioned was a truly necessary manifestation. He saw in it, however, not a weakening but a strengthening of the position of Christ Himself because thereby all nominal following was excluded. As certain as he was that his kerygma would lose all meaning without the fact of the resurrection of Jesus or, as he says, would become "vain" (1 Cor. 15:14), so immovably firm did the resurrection of Jesus stand for him (1 Cor. 15:20). But it was not immovably certain for him only because he had seen the Risen One himself (1 Cor. 15:8; 9:1), but above all, because he had experienced the Crucified One as the Living One in his life and in Him had learned to know God's power to save and had also experienced the same in all others who "believe." (1 Cor. 1:18, 24; cf. Rom. 1:16)

From the formula "power of God for salvation" it follows

with perfect clarity that the nature of the apostolic concern is practical and not theoretical. The goal of the apostles was not to convey knowledge and religious theories and through them to provide men with the possibility of arming themselves against all contingencies of life and of making themselves independent of them. The apostles strove for the καινότης ζωῆς (Rom. 6:4), which comes about through the forgiveness of sins and the granting of fellowship with the living Christ. With this goal all moral and religious ideals of the time were surpassed, not because a new, more sharply defined ideal was placed beside them but because it can be said on the basis of the resurrection of Jesus: "If anyone is in Christ, he is a new creation. The old has passed away; behold, the new one has come" (2 Cor. 5:17). This, however, was not only said; rather, everyone who wanted to could experience it. That the congregations also experienced it emerges from the fact that the formula "the saints" is one of the most important self-designations of the ancient Christians. It testifies that they really were under the sovereignty of Jesus and found the enriching of their life in the fact that they had become "new" through Him. It is important to reach clarity on this point because only then do we see that the apostolic proclamation of Jesus as the goal of the history of humanity and of life for every individual person was more than a word — that it came from life and reality and therefore led to life and reality.

If we take a look from this point of view into the present-day world, we find that it has long since been a part of the heaviest woes under which the incumbent of the office of the ministry groans that the unconditional observance of the unconditional indicative is upheld by the church today only theoretically and not also practically. Without trying to suggest that any particular ecclesiastical or religious group should or could be blamed, it must be admitted that during the course of the last two centuries and especially during the last decades the church in wide circles has abandoned the claim of absoluteness for its message. One need only recall the doctrinal developments before the war and it at once becomes obvious that the official church has given up its positions step by step. But in this the mistake lies much less in a more or less clearly stated abandonment of this or that theological position than in an attitude not exclusively determined by the recognition that the representation of Jesus gives meaning to the ecclesiastical office and that the testimony to Him as the Coming One gives meaning to the church. The mistake lies in an attitude which besides this allows room for still other important factors.

To these factors belongs in the first place consideration for the religious man who cannot accept the ecclesiastical proclamation in its totality. There has been reluctance to draw the boundaries as sharply as possible and a readiness rather to accept the division than give up clear fronts. And this, sad to say, has come about partly on the basis of motives that are not very spiritual. The blame falls especially on those who through the Lord of the office and their affirmative answer to His will are appointed to hold the fort and who yet say no to the advancement of His front. All of us have failed time and again to continue declaring with justified and necessary emphasis that not the merely religious man but only the man who has been overcome by the crucified and risen Christ and who is of service to the living and coming Christ enjoys God's goodwill and has attained the goal set for him by God. We have fallen into the same error not only in the case of individuals but as far as our entire nation is concerned. Hence it is not a coincidence and consequently also in no way only an invention of the enemies of the church but directly based on a widespread attitude of the official church and on a common attitude of the incumbents of the ecclesiastical office that the impression has arisen in an increasing degree that the church with its proclamation and worship is certainly an important—perhaps even the most important—factor for our nation and its members. But it is also felt that besides the church there are other factors with equally basic rights and that it depends entirely on the individual from what quarter he feels he is being addressed and where he finds satisfaction for his religious needs. Anyone who has some idea of the situation knows that these statements summarize the viewpoint of the most widespread circles among our people.

Where are the deepest roots of this attitude to be found, an attitude that presents itself to us with more difficulty every passing day? Are they to be sought in a fateful emancipation of the West from ecclesiastical authority, which is to be traced back to the Reformation? Or do they actually lie within the church? If we want to bring about a change here, the only thing that can help is complete honesty and clarity and the abandonment of all apologetics simply for the sake of principle. Such an abandonment will certainly bear fruit for the church and its work through the office of the church. We follow the way where the blame is first sought in ourselves and not in others, and we shall go a little farther along this way in company with S. Kierkegaard.

In his writing already mentioned[114] *Of the Difference Between a Genius and an Apostle* Kierkegaard found the decline of the religious authority of the preachers already in his time in the fact that they delivered "profound" lectures instead of passing on in thetical form what is given to them in the Word of Jesus and what is answered by Him. He elucidates the attitude of the preacher as it should be with the question whether there is an eternal life. His opinion is that "in order to speak correctly a Christian priest would have to say, quite simply: We have Christ's Word for it that there is an eternal life; and that settles the matter. There is no question here of racking one's brains or philosophizing, but simply that Christ said it, not as a profound thinker but with divine authority."[115]

According to Kierkegaard, everything depends on this divine authority, and therefore it is not necessary for Christ to be "profound." We would rather say that because the Crucified One has proved Himself to be the Living One and the One coming again, His words require no substantiation but receive their validity solely and in an adequate degree from the fact that He has spoken them. This distinguishes His words in an essential manner from all other words that have ever been spoken. All other words have to be "profound" to be able to raise any claim to consideration, but precisely for this reason they prove that they do not have divine authority and therefore can be binding only insofar as they are proved to be correct before the forum of critical understanding. "What Plato says on immortality really is profound, reached after deep study; but then poor Plato has no authority whatsoever."[116]

Because Plato spoke as a thinker but Jesus out of the plenitude of power belonging to Him who is the beginning and the end (Rev. 1:17; 2:8; 22:13), Plato founds pupils, but Jesus appointed apostles partly besides and partly among His μαθηταί and established in the apostolic office the office of the representation of Himself in His authority. Therefore Jesus' work in the church also falls apart when the bearers of His office cease to base their office on His authority. Because it belongs to the essence of the Word of Jesus to compel the will to make a decision, no matter whether it is for or against Him, it already amounts to a false representation of His own office and an obscuring of its essence when His representatives in the church's office of the ministry so much as consider the possibility of a discussion concerning the validity or the dimensions of His claim, to say nothing of allowing a discussion of this kind and even taking part in it. It is not the business of an apostle to supply evidence for the rights of his commissioner. Much rather, Jesus covers His representative with His authority, provided that the representative is prepared to expect everything for his office from this authority and nothing from himself. He must not even expect anything from his ruminating mental powers or his clear insight into things, not even from his impeccably scientific and perhaps even ecclesiastically correct theology.

As important as all this is for the incumbent of the office, and as much as it may even be indispensable for him from the viewpoint of the correct discharge of his office, it is nevertheless completely inadequate for establishing his right to bring Christ's will in this age to men so that they may come to a decision, no matter who they may be. In view of the magnitude of the issue at stake, it would moreover be for him a hopeless undertaking to wish to base the claim raised on anything else but the authority of Jesus Himself. There is no way any man can by himself convince another man that he has the duty to remind him of his sins and that he also has the right to proclaim the forgiveness of sins to him in the name of Jesus if he desires it.

The authorization to proclaim the Word, an authorization by which the incumbent carries out his office, is a relationship only between the Lord of the office and himself and not between himself and those whom he approaches with his proclamation and belongs to that which the incumbent of the apostolate as well as of the office of the ministry must accept. At first this may seem to be a heavy burden to him and often makes his proclamation a trying experience. But if he is at this point in earnest about representing Jesus, he will very soon feel how an authorization in fact ensues, an authorization for proclamation as only He can confer who holds all things in His hand. Only if the incumbent in his consciousness of office has freed himself through the Lord of the office from all considerations of men and also from consideration of himself and of the good or bad role which he is playing as the supposed administrator of the Gospel before men, will his proclamation become free of all considerations of the hearer. It will also be freed from all hindrances and ties to which it falls victim only too easily if the one entrusted with the office makes himself and his own person the center of his considerations concerning the office and its administration. All who administer the office of Jesus are subject to this danger, for only too readily we forget the grace vouchsafed to us in Jesus and hence are too easily inclined to trace to our own performance what actually happens despite our imperfections through the Lord of the office in the case of His administrators. Where joy in the proclamation languishes, it does so in the shadow of this danger. For this very reason nothing more important can happen to the incumbent in the interests of the purity of his office and the purity of his proclamation than that he should be freed from the tension between his ego and the objective character of his office through the simple connection of his ego with Him who called him, a sinner, to the office of representing Him, the coming Lord, till He comes.

In the very moment when this tension is overcome the distress so often imparted with the proclamation and felt by many to be coupled with the office will also be overcome. If the Christ Himself is experienced as the Lord of the office who is just as responsible for the office as its incumbent, every dialectical trait also disappears from the proclamation and the full apostolic ring of the testimony to forgiveness *that has been achieved* and complete fellowship with God *as a present possession* in His Christ for all who bow to His claim is secured. If Jesus is the Risen One and the Coming

One and if He has already entered upon His sovereignty and documents it in His representatives, the motto for all proclamation in the church can only be the joyous and thankful yes to His saving and preserving presence. On the same basis it is an obscuring of what has taken place if tension and not the solution of tensions is made the characteristic feature of today's Christian life in the presence of the Coming One. He who knows and wants to know his office as representation of Jesus and nothing else will become certain of that also today and remain certain of it so long as the office of representing Jesus remains in the office of the ministry.

It was no enthusiasm, neither an expression of the experience of one who had received special grace, and certainly not a Christian theory, when Paul exultingly saw in the person who is "in Christ" the old disappearing and the new taking its place (2 Cor. 5:17), but it was and is the testimony of what the Christ does today for those who acknowledge Him, the testimony of what He also does for the nation which bows to His claim. It is time for us to tell this to our nation with the joy of the apostles and to testify that it "pays" to acknowledge the sovereignty of Christ. Our nation has been waiting for this proclamation for a long time. Is this waiting destined to have been in vain because the called incumbents do not have the confidence in the Lord of their office that He still does today what Paul and many others experienced during their lives? The more correct way for them would be to raise the petition of Paul the prisoner as their own petition: "that utterance may be given me in opening my mouth joyfully to proclaim the mystery of the Gospel . . . so that I may be able to act and speak therein with joy, as it is fitting." (Eph. 6:19-20)[117]

With the solution of the tension between his ego and

his office in their relationship to Him who accepts responsibility for and supports the office of representing Himself, the proclamation of the office of the ministry not only receives its New Testament depth but also its New Testament breadth. The universalism of the proclamation of our time in its called bearers of the office takes its place beside the universalism of the apostolate. He would certainly be a poor representative of his Lord in whom His concern is not burning in his soul in such a way that he is ready to go with Him wherever possible and ready to step with Him before all men whether they are Christians, Jews, or heathens. Both office and incumbent who reject this and do not consider mission work, also Jewish mission work, valid, have completely severed their connection with the basis of the office of representing Jesus and thereby also from the basis of the ecclesiastical office and no longer have any right to speak and act in the name of Jesus. Today, no less than was the case with the apostles, one does not take up the office of Jesus to determine its limits by himself; he takes it up only in order to carry out Jesus' commission by subordinating his own will to the will of the sender. This commission reads: "Make disciples of *all* nations" (Matt. 28:19). Over against this commission there can only be obedience or disobedience. One can only be taken up with it or be broken by it.

To be taken up with the idea of service is also ultimately of extreme importance for the attitude of the person entrusted with the office toward the proclamation. He is lifted out of the drudgery of weekly or even daily proclamation and led to joy in it and with it. And this is possible in no other way. It is based on the fact that his proclamation is no longer under the "must" without a corresponding "can" but under what may be claimed as a right. This enters the realm of possibility in Christ, so that the proclamation takes place in collaboration with God's own work, who in Christ still allows the old to pass away and become new and thereby builds His kingdom in the midst of a perverse generation.

CHAPTER 9

The Calling

From what has been said thus far it has become clear in an increasing degree that the office of the ministry has a special, unique character that separates it from all other offices and callings. Its uniqueness lies in the fact that it cannot exist as an office by itself, not even – and this is an essential factor – theoretically, but that it comes into existence only through a man's surrender to Jesus Christ as the Lord of the office.

The situation is not changed by the fact that according to the view of the call held by Martin Luther and Lutheranism every call is from God and hence receives its full meaning only if it is fulfilled as a call from God. It is actually possible to become and to be a worker, an official, an employer, a lawyer, a doctor etc., and to find pleasure in one's work, above all, to do it in these spheres with such perfection as is possible for man without even believing in God at all, to say nothing of receiving his work from God's hand and attributing to Him a determining influence on its form. Hence also a fairly superior attitude is adopted toward these callings. It is possible not only to make a free choice among them, especially if one has the necessary means, but he can also in large measure shape them and fill them with content according to his discretion. It is therefore possible, whether one is a worker, an official, or follows a free calling, to see in his calling first and foremost the basis of his outward existence. It can be looked at solely from the viewpoint of monetary gain. It can be accepted as a necessary evil, but one can also fulfill it in love and with sacrifice; in short, it is possible here, basically and irrespective of every religious standpoint, to consider one's lifework and vocation in isolation, to interpret it by himself, to give it form by himself, and to adopt such an attitude toward it that he stands at the center of it in his own person and from this center sets about his calling in a really sober manner. Not all may do this, and it may not always be as simple as it appears; but no one who has ever made observations on these matters or reflected on them will deny that the actual relationship of person and calling that has been here set forth is possible if separation and demarcation of personal interests and the interests of one's calling takes place. And this often enough appears in actual fact without the calling suffering harm thereby or being compelled to suffer harm.

Such an attitude toward his calling is impossible for one who administers the office of the ministry. It is a part of the very essence of the office of the ministry that the personality becomes completely absorbed by the office and that this absorption takes place to such an extent that every form of existence outside the office ceases, even that of a most personal nature. If an attitude is developed in which the incumbent emancipates himself from his office even only for a time, he ceases to be an incumbent in the sense that he is adminstering the office of representing Jesus. A man occupies the office of representing Jesus only for so long as the authority of Jesus covers him and supports him. This authority, however, is withdrawn from him by the Lord of the office when he departs from the apostolic basis of his office by ceasing to allow his office and therefore the Lord of the office to be the sole principle of his attitude to life and the ordering of his life. As an incumbent he lives solely from his connection with the Lord of his office and in the realization of this connection in his life, which has found eternal meaning, content, and worth in the office. For the life of the incumbent, which becomes merged in his office, and for his office, which makes a total claim on his life, all depends on his personal relationship with the Lord of his office.

It is only a case of describing this state of affairs in other words when one says: The office is derived only from the call issued to the one designated for office and from the decision by which submission to the call to office takes place. Here all the stress lies on the call. In the concept of the call is included the idea that there is no other answer possible for him to whom it is issued but the affirmative decision. To this extent the call to the office of representing the Christ and the decision in favor of this call are one and the same act of God. What the one entrusted with the office is, he is through his call to office; and what he becomes in his office, he likewise becomes through this call. So long as he holds the office, there is no moment in his life when he does not feel obliged to live and carry out his office only from the basis of his calling. And if he knows what his office really is, he will also live it and discharge it alone.

Hence it is not only consistent but indispensable that the call to office be the decisive experience in the life of the New Testament apostles, beside which nothing can stand comparison. Here we find the roots of their efficient workmanship as well as their humility. From this source flows the power for the total fulfillment of their commission, presenting a graphic description of the present and the coming Christ. And this they do as men bound to space and time and continually threatened by sin. This is also the source whence the power is derived to suffer all in the fulfillment of their commission and even to accept persecution and death for His sake without being aware of anything else but praise and thanks for what they must still regard as grace from the Lord of the office in the event of suffering and death for the sake of their commission.

This again is set forth most clearly in Paul.[118] For us he is also the classical representative of the apostolate because in none of the New Testament apostles is the meaning of the call for the apostle's consciousness of office and for the discharge of his commission so clearly recognizable as in his case. The apostle Paul and his experience near Damascus, which he himself understood as a personal encounter with the Risen One, or, more correctly, as a personal encounter of the Risen One with himself – an experience which he esteemed as his most precious possession – cannot be outwardly separated from each other, not even from the viewpoint of the critical observer, unless the apostle ceases to be an apostle.

We are not going to repeat what has already been said earlier [119] on the character of Paul's Damascus experience as the hour of decision. On the other hand we must not fail to show how for Paul his whole life and work in his call to the office of an apostle is established by Christ Himself. To realize this, it is enough to refer once again to what has already been mentioned,[120] namely, the manner in which he judged and appraised the sufferings his office brought upon him. This manner has its ultimate basis in Paul's certainty of his call. Without this it would have been unthinkable that in all his persecutions and dangers and in the innumerable hindrances with which he had to contend continuously Paul could have seen anything but what everyone else would have been compelled to see in them: the burdening of his outward and the embitterment of his inner life. But Paul viewed all this, as well as his life in general, in the light of his calling, and so for him his sufferings as an apostle became the opposite of a burden that would benumb his joy in office. They became the confirmation of his office for himself as well as for his congregations.

The central position of the call in Paul's consciousness of office and in the administration of his office is underlined meanwhile when one notes his abrupt refusal of all attempts to set up a basis for his office that does not stem directly from the certainty of his call. Above all, it is a question of rejecting every attempt to establish the apostolic authority by way of the possession of special ecstatic experiences and to secure it against every attack. The classic passage is 2 Cor. 12:1-10.[121] With clear insight into the essence of his office and imbued with the conclusive and sufficient character of his call, Paul separates himself from his opponents, who made a great show of their ecstatic experiences and sought to put him in the shade by relating them. He clearly recognized the danger threatening the apostolate and every form of "official" authority in the congregation on this score. If the wealth or the dearth of visions and divine inner voices, for which there was inclination at least in the Greek congregations, is made the standard for measuring the claims of the bearers of the office to authority, and whether the claim is affirmed or rejected, the office would be imperiled in its innermost essence. In that case the cult of the pious personality would have emerged anew, the precise thing of which Jesus had made a clean sweep. Basically it does not matter whether the veneration of human achievement is the basis of such a cult, as Jesus confronted it in the rabbinate, or the veneration of the pneumatic. The decisive factor is that in both instances the danger of deception and self-deception is present and that the office would necessarily lose its objective character if the way were opened for either one. This would apply to the incumbent himself as well as to those for whom the office is intended. It would become dependent on human judgment and thereby forfeit without further ado the right to raise the claim of absoluteness.

Paul's radical delimitation of the apostolate over against enthusiasm reaches deep and far beyond the advocacy of a mere theory of office. Especially Paul, who advocated it so emphatically, could have made a boast of ecstatic experiences in special measure (besides 2 Cor. 12:1-4 see 1 Cor. 14:18) and therefore would have had no cause to avoid in this area an encounter and also comparison with his opponents. When he nevertheless declined to do so, he followed this course for the sake of his office, whose independence from every human factor (see besides Gal. 1:1 especially 1 Cor. 4:3) was more important to him and to every true apostle than the importance of his own personality. For Paul, however, the independence of his office was assured only through his call and through the binding that took place in him of his own person to the Lord of the office.

Thus the call necessarily occupies a place at the center of the apostolic consciousness of office. It is true that this does not mean a safeguarding of the claim outwardly. It is not possible for the apostle to supply unequivocal evidence obvious to everyone for the claim with which he appears on the scene. Is it not a weakening of his office when this is impossible? Only he will think so who fails to see that the same decision which must be made concerning the Lord of the office must also be reached in the case of His representative. It belongs to the essence of the apostolic office as the office of representing Jesus that one either "believes" its administrator or not, for no third possibility exists as far as taking a position is concerned. "If he could prove it *physically* [the possession of the authority claimed] then he would not be an Apostle. He has no other proof than his own statement. That has to be so; for otherwise the believer's relationship to him would be direct instead of being paradoxical. . . . An Apostle has no other proof than his own statement, and at the most his willingness to suffer anything for the sake of that statement." [122]

Viewed from the office and its basis the fact that the apostle is rooted in his calling means strength and not weakness. As one whose life and activity rest solely on the fact of being called, and indeed on being called by the Risen One and the One who is returning, he is freed inwardly and outwardly from all ties which men could and would impose on him if his claim could actually be the subject of a basic discussion, to say nothing of supplying evidence with all logical means. Hence he becomes free to carry out his task in the universal manner in which Christ carried out His task and in the same freedom from men and in the same dependence on the Giver of the office which was the characteristic of His activity.

So far we have spoken only of Paul, yet we have left no doubt that in speaking of him we have spoken of all the apostles. That we were right in simply assuming the central significance of the call for his consciousness of office and also for his activity, is demonstrated by the wording of all the Easter reports of the New Testament. "In Paul the Easter history [123] is placed exclusively under the viewpoint that Jesus provided Himself with messengers through it." [124] But this does not happen as the result of a special situation in which he found himself when he came to speak about the resurrection of Jesus. His method of connecting the resurrection of Jesus and his own call into office with each other is certainly the method also of the others who furnish an account.

> In Matthew the mission of the disciples is the kernel of the whole account. In Luke the journey of Jesus with the two disciples to Emmaus portrays Him as the comforter of His own who again helps them to faith, but the aim of the Easter history also in Luke is the founding of the apostolate. In John the chief part of his Easter account directly serves his central thought. He shows how the Risen One united the disciples with Himself by faith and gave them the authority for their work. But the second part [125] also . . .

stands beneath the important consciousness of office of the first part.[126]

Nothing could more clearly set forth the central significance of the call to office for the apostle and for the church, in the confines of which he does his work, than the portrayal of the Easter event in the light of the calling of men into His service, as it may be observed in the account. If the apostle cannot bear witness to the Risen One without at the same time bearing witness to his calling, then the only conceivable thing is that his whole life in office is supported and given form by the call to office.

An important factor under these circumstances is that we find the same estimate of the call in Luther, and in a manner that is directly related to the apostles. It is true that in the case of the apostles it was not a question of the same meaning that the call into the office of the ministry had for Luther, but of the meaning it had for him – that he was conscious of being called into his work as a reformer. That Luther's call and Paul's call are very different in their structure makes no difference concerning the fact that Luther's estimate of the call is one with that of Paul.[127] In the case of Paul the entrance into the office of Jesus takes place in a single moment that is decisive above everything else.[128] But Luther was led to the turning-point in his life in a continuous movement that extended over 15 years, on the basis of which he began the reformatory work that was to supply him with content and distinctive features for his work.[129] This difference is based in part on the fact that in the former instance it is a case of "conversion and calling *to* Christianity," whereas in the latter instance it is "conversion and calling *in* Christianity."[130] It also rests on the fact that Luther's call would not be conceivable without the figure of a Paul called to be an apostle. Finally, one should perhaps also take into consideration that in Paul and Luther the given presuppositions of calling in the relationship of the one not yet called to God do not coincide and therefore each operates in a different way from the other in the calling.[131] The difference in both cases can be emphasized as sharply as possible, and in doing so we get a stronger impression of the common bond between Luther and Paul in the manner in which they prized their call and made it the basis of their whole work. Like Paul, time and again Luther gained the strength to bear his office from the certainty of his call by God or by Jesus Himself and from no other source.

Out of the large number of passages that could be cited in proof of this statement we offer only two especially telling statements by Luther.[132] The one belongs to the days of the Diet of Augsburg. At that time, as was often the case also at other times, Luther experienced the ardent desire that he could be a private individual rather than a man on whom all eyes were focused. But he knew and said that this would not only be impossible "for the sake of the poor souls" who waited upon his word but especially for the sake of Him who had appointed him to his position. "Besides there is also a man named Jesus Christ who says 'No' to my resignation. I rightly follow Him to whom I am even more indebted." [133] Here it is not just Luther's sense of duty [134] over against the task that finds expression, but the same thought that Paul expresses in 1 Cor. 9:16: "Woe to me if I do not preach the Gospel!"

That the passage cited from Luther is to be understood only in this sense is shown by another passage in which he expresses his view on his call to be a reformer:

> Had I known about it beforehand, He (God) would have had to take more pains to get me in. Be that as it may, I intend to perform the duties of the office with His help. On account of the exceedingly great and heavy cares and

> worries connected with it, I would not take the whole world to enter upon this work now. On the other hand, when I regard Him who called me, I would not take the whole world not to have begun it.[135]

Here all the weight lies on his being called in such a way that in his call he recognizes and acknowledges the meaning of his life.

Although this thought is completely apostolic and also truly Pauline, the apostolic character of Luther's consciousness of his call receives its confirmation from a number of other factors. Among them special mention must be made of the magnitude of his claim. Luther occasionally called himself "the prophet of the Germans" and also "one of the apostles and evangelists in the land of the Germans."[136] In the midst of the serious discussions of the year 1521 he writes: "Even if it were true that I alone had brought myself to the fore, they would still not be excused thereby. Who knows if God has not called and raised me for this purpose and if it is not to be feared in their case that they are despising God in me? Do we not read that God generally raised up only one prophet at a time in the Old Testament?"[137]

Here a certainty of being called emerges in a magnitude to be found, except for Luther, only in the New Testament apostles. Attention should also be paid to a common clarity of consciousness. Luther is "the one great figure in Christianity who did not appeal to a vision or some other extraordinary contact with the heavenly world."[138] In this respect he takes up a position beside Paul, whose life was rich in ecstatic experiences but who never used them to make his office and authority secure with their help and thus make them dependent on such experiences. Neither of them had to do this because they were conscious of being called, and therefore their office stood on an immovable foundation. For Luther the decisive rejection of enthusiasm and its claims based on special revelations lay in the consequences drawn from this fact.[139]

All these facts are of great importance for Luther's concept of office and its basis. This may be said, although we have in them in the first instance only his view of the importance of the call for his own office and not for the office of the ministry in general. That we do not have here a conscious isolation of his office from the office of a pastor emerges already in his occasional comparison not only of himself but also of Melanchthon to Jeremiah,[140] whose figure had such a strong influence on the formation of a consciousness of mission and calling in Paul.[141] Luther thus attributed a calling and a commission also to his friend and collaborator, although the latter was never called in the manner of Luther himself. Had it been otherwise, he would never have been able to compare Melanchthon to a prophet, and least of all to the classic example of a prophet so conscious of his mission as was Jeremiah. Since this is nevertheless done, it means that Luther's attitude toward the call to office through the Lord of history and the valuation of the call as the basis of the functions of the office are present in him in personal form but as far as content is concerned are not limited to his person or to his special situation. This is established, moreover, by the statements from the beginning of the large commentary of Galatians discussed in an earlier context.[142] They hang completely in the air if we do not grant validity to the call to office through the Lord of the office as *the* basis also for the consciousness and certainty of office and also for the joy derived from the office by the administrator of the one in the office of the ministry.

The question still remains why Luther did not express this more clearly. It remains all the more because the lack of systematic statements by Luther indicating course and direction proved to be a great hindrance to the development of a healthy consciousness of office in the realm of the evangelical church. Luther's silence is to some extent understandable because of the situation in which he found himself. As far as the concept of office was concerned, he had to battle on two fronts: that of the Catholic Church with its sacrament of priestly ordination and a concept of office bordering on the sacramental, and that of the *Schwärmer* with their enthusiasm, which naturally banned the office above all else. In both cases ideas were current that could easily be applied to the formula of "calling," but always in such a way that the New Testament and apostolic idea of calling to office was neglected or left completely out of consideration. And this is also the case with the *character indelebilis* (the indelible character) of the Roman priest as well as with the *Schwärmer,* for in both cases a regular office in the long run proved to be impossible because the New Testament and apostolic idea of service combined with the calling was simply not granted its rights.

Luther must be understood in this light when he placed the emphasis in the call into the ministry on the part played by the ecclesiastical government and ecclesiastical law in the calling, but without wanting to diminish or even set aside its inner significance for the bearer of the office who is about to commence his duties. And we have no grounds for blaming him on this score. We nevertheless still labor under the inheritance from the Reformation and try to understand ordination in the traditional manner predominantly as a juridical action. In our day, when the question concerning the spiritual authority of the bearer of the office within and outside the church and especially among the clergy themselves has broken out anew, we labor even harder than was the case already in the middle of the last century in the Lutheran Church when it was influenced by a newly awakened consciousness of office. No less a figure than L. A. Petri at that time repeatedly raised the demand in his new publication and elsewhere for an inner and outer reorganization of ordination and made proposals in this direction.[143] What moved him to do this was not a liturgical problem but consideration for the administrators of the office of the ministry at the commencement of their duties and the relatively small significance ordination in general had for them. It is characteristic that he did not approach the ecclesiastical government with a program but spoke his mind when confronted by present and future brethren in office on the essential nature of ordination and what it should therefore mean to them. It should be the hour for making a simple decision for the Lord of the office and His commission and the hour for receiving His authorization. It is also the hour in which the whole of the future life in office receives content and the bearer of the office who is commencing his duties is received into the service of the Coming One. These were fruitful approaches, but they remained approaches.

The question is whether we must now move forward at all costs for the sake of the office. We have seen how the apostolic office of representing Jesus lives on in the office of the church as the office of the present and returning Christ, and we have seen that there is no way leading to Him except that of absolute decision for the Lord of the office and His commission. All presuppositions for a consciousness of office, a certainty of office, and a rejoicing in office by the one entrusted with the ministry, which was characteristic of the apostles, are herewith supplied. And with them the way is prepared for overcoming a false consciousness of office — either spiritual presumption and pride of place or else falsely placed humility. Only one thing is missing for bringing about such an apostolic consciousness in our pastors in regard to their office, and that is an hour in which they consciously come to a decision for the way of the apostles, an hour in which absolute clarity is achieved between the Lord of the office and its bearer also in the direction as to what the bearer of the office may expect from his Lord. In short, what is needed is an hour corresponding to the hour of the call into the apostolate and an hour in which everything included under the perspective of being called into office through the Lord of the church is once again brought together from its beginning. This includes everything that has long since engaged the attention of him who is aspiring to office, or at least should have engaged his attention.

This hour presents itself in ordination. The only task is to fashion it anew as to its form and content. This needs to be done on the basis of a new consciousness of its essence in connection with the new consciousness of the essence of the office of the ministry. This must be the man's hour of decision for the office of Christ, for which he is brought to a decision through the will of Christ.

From the viewpoint of the apostolic office, how do matters stand with the man who desires the office of the ministry?

> He approaches as a freeman but becomes a slave in body and soul and all that he has. For the one to whom the office is entrusted becomes a servant of Christ and takes his Lord's yoke upon himself in a different sense from the rest of the believers. Henceforth he wants to live under contract to this Lord. His thinking, loving, and willing is to be merged in the cause of this Lord. His soul must live in this cause, his members must be offered in its service. What he has gained and gains daily in knowledge, wisdom, experience, in skill and power he is prepared to expend on this cause. For it he is prepared to have time, for everything else none. This cause he will pursue and become its slave and remain free from all other services and activities. For it he will live and not know people, wife and child, brothers and sisters in carrying it out and fear neither the world nor its rulers. With this cause he will pass through honor and disgrace, through good and evil reports. For this cause he will work, watch, pray, fight, fall, and

die to the praise, glory, and honor of Him who called him, regarded him as faithful, placed him in office, loved him, and gave Himself for him.[144]

The correct consciousness of office is knowing all this and acting according to it every hour and at every opportunity. No one is prevented from stretching out his hand toward the office. But he who reaches for it should know what he wants to receive and should give ear to the words "we shall be judged with greater strictness" (James 3:1). And when he has heard this, he must not forget it and will not forget it. For to know that the office comes into being by the call through the Christ means to know that the administration of the office means to live from the call. Otherwise the office comes to its end before it has begun, for then it is no longer the office of Jesus.

If we have this understanding of ordination, it serves to make the way to office more difficult. We have no reason to suppose that this would not have met with Luther's approval, who was as conscious of the magnitude of the office as he was of the shortcomings of its administrators in the face of its magnitude.

Regarded in this way, ordination furthermore unites all those called to office in the brotherhood of those who have surrendered themselves and all that they have to the Christ so that His business may go forward. Brotherhood is not possible on the basis of a calling along the lines common in our midst, and the pastoral office has been largely reduced to this by our fault. But brotherhood develops where all surrender to the One and stand in His service. The relationship of brethren in office as it should be but is not has belonged to the painful phenomena of the Protestant setup already for centuries and is responsible for a greater breakdown in the work of the church and the representation of the wishes of Christ than is generally supposed. The reciprocal comparisons, rivalries, and struggles will come to an end only where the form of the Lord of the office with His promises and threats alike stands before all those who administer His office through His call. The Lord, however, stands in the hour of ordination – understood in the apostolic sense of calling and decision – before each one and goes with him into the office and all the way through the office. And He either tears him away from himself to make him free for service to Himself or He refuses to validate him and thereby separates his office from His own office. That they were all called by the same Lord welded the apostles of Jesus Christ into a unity despite their differences.[145] This is also possible today if the common basis of office is understood as clearly as the apostles did. There is no question that Luther would have here given his unqualified affirmation on the basis of what he thought and said about his office.

The most important thing emerging from the new conception of ordination is that it obligates the one who accepts the office to remain in constant association with the Lord of the office. Only in such constant association is it possible to reach the constantly new validation which the bearer of the office requires for carrying out his commission to represent the Christ "between the times." Under these circumstances all depends on his decision how things must be done and what must be done and left undone. Here again the apostles of the New Testament are the great examples for those who continue their office – Jesus' own office – in the office of the ministry. Paul, to name only one of them, stands where we always meet him, ἀδιαλείπτως in his relationship with the Christ. But here we also stand on the summit and at the same time on the boundary of what can actually be said concerning the office of the church, its essence, and its basis from the perspective of the apostolate, for "this is a chapter with which we can come to grips best of all in our private room. And the present time certainly requires us to make diligent use of this room. From there we must bring with us . . . a reflection on our countenance, of which it may be said: 'And gazing at him, all who sat in the council saw that his face was like the face of an angel.' This of course is no protection against the stones, but it is a validation of the servant of Christ and smites his foes."[146]

Before this reflection, we may add, the mocking question as to how just this man or that one happened to come forward with the claim to be able to forgive the sins of men in God's name is silenced.[147] Or the question may change into the hatred of an open decision against Christ and His representatives. In the face of this situation it is again proved true that even today it is not the ecclesiastical authorities, neither the ecclesiastical organizations and their associations, nor the representatives of a correct theology and proclamation but only the fervid hearts that have been surrendered to the Lord of the office which fight and win the battles of God.

Notes

1. Rudolf Bultmann and others, *Krisis des Glaubens, Krisis der Kirche, Krisis der Religion* (Giessen, 1931), p. 17.
2. As a typical witness mention may be made of *Tagebuch eines Grossstadtpfarrers* (Berlin, 1929 ff.), p. 27 et passim.
3. For the actual state of affairs see the brief remarks by F. Niebergall in *Die Religion in Geschichte und Gegenwart,* 2d ed. (Tübingen, 1927), I, col. 865.
4. In conformity with the theme, by "ecclesiastical office" here and in what follows is always meant the office of one who is *rite vocatus.*
5. This has rightly been stressed by J. Kögel in *Das geistliche Amt im Neuen Testament und in der Gegenwart* (Dresden, 1929), pp. 7 ff.
6. See, for example, C. Weizsäcker, *Das apostolische Zeitalter der christlichen Kirche,* 3d ed. (Tübingen, 1902), pp. 616, 618 ff.; Adolf Schlatter, *The Church in the New Testament Period,* trans. Paul P. Levertoff (London: S. P. C. K., 1961), pp. 76 ff.
7. So also Kögel, *Das geistliche Amt,* etc., p. 7. Kögel, by the way, deliberately leaves the presbytery out of consideration.
8. Apart from 1 Cor. 15:9 ("unfit to be called an apostle") see especially Eph. 2:20, where the (New Testament) apostles form the foundation of the congregation before the (Old Testament) prophets. See my observations in *Theological Dictionary of the New Testament,* ed. Gerhard Kittel, trans. Geoffrey W. Bromiley (Grand Rapids: Eerdmans, 1964—), I, 440 ff., under ἀπόστολος. Hereafter cited as TD.
9. See here and especially in what follows my investigation of the term ἀπόστολος, ibid, pp. 407 ff.
10. For the relation of apostle and teacher in early Christianity see my reflections, ibid., II, 146, 157 ff., under διδάσκω, etc.
11. P. W. Schmiedel finds "a more exact gradation of rank" in 1 Cor. 12:28 in his *Hand-Commentar zum NT.,* 2d ed. (Freiburg, 1892), II 1, 170. Ph. Bachmann adopts a similar view in *Der erste Brief*

des Paulus an die Korinther (Leipzig, 1903), p. 395, note 2 among others.

12. Kögel found the three factors which determine the essence of the Christian office for all time in the Spirit, the congregation, and the Word (*Das geistliche Amt,* etc., pp. 8 ff.). This important recognition will be taken for granted in the following discussions but, on the basis of the results of historical linguistics, will be extended and deepened.
13. This is also Kögel's view, p. 7.
14. See, for example, B. E. Klostermann, *Das Lukasevangelium,* 2d ed. (Tübingen, 1929), p. 77, on this passage.
15. See my investigation of ἀπόστολος, TD, I, 413 ff.
16. 1 Sam. 25:39 ff; 2 Sam. 10:1 ff. See also my investigation, TD, I, 414 ff.
17. *Mischna Beradot,* 5, 5 et passim.
18. Examples of this as well as for the following are found in TD, I, 415.
19. Here cf. Tobith 7:13: "And he called his wife Edna, took a page and wrote the marriage settlement (συγγραφή), and they [i. e., the witnesses to the marriage; cf. here my *Jebamot* (Giessen, 1929), p. 51] signed their names."
20. In Judaism the act that establishes marriage is not the wedding with which the transfer to the husband's house is connected, but the betrothal. Cf. Matt. 1:18 ff., and Deut. 22:23 ff.
21. Deut. 24:1 ff. and *Mischna Jebamot,* 4:12: "If a man takes his divorced wife to himself again . . . he must separate himself from her, and the child is a bastard."
22. Further examples, ibid.
23. See the examples in TD, I, 416.
24. See the examples, ibid., pp. 419 ff.
25. This is also valid in the case of a vicarious betrothal. See *Mischna Kidduschin,* 3, 1: "If a man says to his companion, 'Go and betroth such and such a woman to me,' and he goes and betroths her to himself, she is betrothed to the second man."
26. *Numeri rabba,* 16, 1, on 13:2.
27. On Gal. 1:1.
28. "Slias" from "schelicha," like "Messias" from "meschicha."
29. See the many futures in Matt. 10:16 ff.
30. In Matt. 10:19 ff. Jesus does not promise His messengers a word that would bring about their acquittal, but the Word with which

the apostle efficaciously proves himself as an emissary and ambassador of Jesus also in a hopeless situation.

31. After what has been said above, we can now venture to use this word.

32. Cf. pp. 39 ff.

33. Cf. also 1 Cor. 7:25. There is, moreover, support for Paul as the author of 1 Tim. to be derived from the fact that here we find the same genuine Pauline attitude: χάριν ἔχω τῷ ἐνδυναμώσαντί με Χριστῷ Ἰησοῦ τῷ κυρίῳ ἡμῶν, ὅτι πιστόν με ἡγήσατο θέμενος εἰς διακονίαν. (1 Tim. 1:12)

34. See my detailed account in TD, I, 424 ff. I do not even have reason on the basis of the prehistory of the apostolate nor on the basis of tradition to doubt that Jesus conferred on His disciples the name of apostle insofar as He called them to take part in His work (cf. TD, I, 427 ff.).

35. This is the case in Matt. 10:5 ff. and parallels. Correspondingly, after the return of the disciples to Jesus, that is, after the fulfillment of their commission as apostles, their designation as such also disappears (cf. Mark 6:30 ff. In Matthew the return is not especially reported, but a corresponding attitude toward the word "apostle" is found here. For Luke's attitude see TD, I, 428 ff.).

36. In spite of the skepticism of R. Bultmann, *Die Geschichte der synoptischen Tradition,* 2d ed. (Göttingen, 1931), pp. 23 ff., this must be insisted on. The ἐν τῷ ὀνόματί σου (Mark) or ἐπὶ τῷ ὀνόματί σου is not in the first place a reference to the use of the ὄνομα of Jesus in the expulsion of demons but to the origin of the authority that comes to light in a miracle.

37. Note that the offense of the disciples is not because of miracles as such but because the strange exorcist arrogates to himself the role of an apostle of Jesus without being one. See Luke 9:49: ὅτι οὐκ ἀκολουθεῖ μεθ' ἡμῶν.

38. See my investigation in TD, I, 430 ff.

39. Note the very significant formula σημεῖα τοῦ ἀποστόλου (2 Cor. 12:12). These "signs by which one recognizes the apostle" are indispensable for Paul for the sake of the matter itself and hence for Jesus' sake, but only insofar as he stands there for Jesus' sake and also for his own sake.

40. See TD, I, 437 ff., and especially Acts 1:21 ff.

41. See Gal. 1:11 ff.

42. See p. 31.

43. Note the τί in 1 Cor. 3:5, which is unavoidable as soon as the apostle is considered without regard for the One who commissioned him. Out of a realization of the same factor Paul in 1 Cor. 1:11 ff.

rejects as a misunderstanding and misuse of the apostolic office the effort to make him and other heralds of the Gospel authorities for individual Christian groups: μὴ Παῦλος ἐσταυρώθη ὑπὲρ ὑμῶν, ἢ εἰς τὸ ὄνομα Παύλου ἐβαπτίσθητε.

44. See note 36.

45. Here alongside λόγος stands ἔργον, signifying exactly what is stated in Gal. 2:8.

46. It is true, and this is very significant for Paul, that he begins to speak of the σημεῖα τοῦ ἀποστόλου (2 Cor. 12:12) when he finds it necessary to offer a self-defense or when there is need of this on pastoral grounds, but never to put his own person into the correct light. See here my investigation in TD, I, 440, and note 39.

47. It is only necessary to compare the combining of his apostolic office with the divine plan of salvation in his consciousness of election (see here TD, I, 441 ff.) as well as the meaning which the form of Jeremiah attained in the expression of the consciousness of his mission (see here TD, I, 439 ff.).

48. Self-evidently, in practice it is impossible to divide the one from the other as is being done here in an intentional schematization. On the basis of the concept of the שָׁלִיחַ (see pp. 25 ff.) it belongs to the essence of an apostle that no possibility exists for him to distinguish between a personal and an official part of his life.

49. Cf. both the attitude of Peter and John in Acts 4:19 ff. and that of Paul (and Barnabas) in Acts 14:8 ff., and especially 2 Cor. 12:1 ff. after 11:16 ff.

50. See 1 Cor. 9:19 ff.

51. As He did it through Christ.

52. The second ὑπέρ should be carried beyond the first inasmuch as the δεόμεθα in v. 20 in a much higher degree than the πρεσβεύομεν stresses the apostle's initiative and in addition the reconciliation is the subject of the proclamation that is God's goal in Christ. Linguistically the different rendering of ὑπέρ offers no difficulty.

53. See E. Fuchs, *Christus und der Geist bei Paulus* (Leipzig, 1932), p. 79.

54. For the power of this consciousness cf. with Gal. 1:6, where the καλέσας is none other than Paul himself, for example, the formula ἕτερον εὐαγγέλιον, ὃ οὐκ ἔστιν ἄλλο (at this very place), with which Paul rejects the proclamation of his opponents. This also wants to be εὐαγγέλιον but is not such because by its nature it is not in accord with Christ. Or cf. the bold statement in 1 Cor. 5:3 ff.

55. One could mention Luther. More on this below.

56. See G. Kittel, "Die Stellung des Jakobus zu Judentum und Heidenchristentum," ZNW, 30 (Giessen, 1931), 145 ff.

57. It appears that he held the office of an apostle (see 1 Cor. 9:5 ff. and also H. Lietzmann, *An die Korinther,* 2d ed. [Tübingen, 1931] on this passage as well as J. Wellhausen, *Nachrichten der kgl. Gesellschaft der Wissenschaften zu Göttingen* [Berlin, 1907], p. 5, note 1), without us knowing when he received it.

58. This would have been a complete expression of the matter if a part of his life's work had actually availed for the Jews of Babylon, as A. Schlatter thinks on the basis of 1 Peter 5:13 (see *Erläuterungen zum Neuen Testament* on this passage; *Die Geschichte der ersten Christenheit* [Gütersloh, 1926], pp. 299 ff.).

59. Perhaps he was active in Corinth (see 1 Cor. 1:12), and toward the end of his life in Rome for certain.

60. Note here in addition Paul's description of himself as a θεοῦ συνεργός in 1 Cor. 3:9, to which the συνεργεῖν with Christ in 2 Cor. 6:1 is to be added. He also concedes this honor to Timothy (1 Thess. 3:2, D* 33 Ambrosiaster). See also the words of Jesus, Matt. 10:40; Luke 10:16.

61. There is no reason for doing so if one reads the account against its historical background.

62. This is in agreement with Matt. 10:19; cf. note 30.

63. The question whether he belonged to the wider circle of the apostles cannot be decided. For the basic question see my investigation in TD, I, 431.

64. These sentences presuppose an explanation of Phil. 3:12 that varies considerably from the one generally offered. The passage does not concern itself with the righteousness of Paul, which is still imperfect and therefore striven after all the more ardently. The thought of δικαιοσύνη is certainly suggested in v. 9, but is not carried any farther. The object of ἔλαβον, moreover, must be taken from the immediate context. As such, v. 10 offers the statement: συμμορφίζεσθαι τῷ θανάτῳ αὐτοῦ or συμμορφίζεσθαι αὐτῷ. The promise of this Paul has in the ἐφ' ᾧ καὶ κατελήμφθην ὑπὸ Χριστοῦ Ἰησοῦ.

65. Their distinguishing feature is that they call themselves apostles but prove by their conduct that they are not (see 2 Cor. 11:13; Rev. 2:2).

66. At least reference needs to be made here to the treatment on the essence of the apostolate by Sören Kierkegaard, *Of the Difference Between a Genius and an Apostle,* bound together with his *The Present Age* (Harper Torchbook, 1962), pp. 87—108. It reaches its climax in the statement: "An Apostle is what he

is by his divine authority" (p. 91). It is in conformity with this when he goes on to say that the business of an apostle is to execute the task laid upon him, which consists in proclaiming the doctrine and using the authority imparted to him — nothing more (p. 106). Here Kierkegaard, without examining the significant historical background of the name apostle, came to a meaning of the apostolate related to ours and which now finds surprising confirmation on linguistic grounds.

67. It was shown above that the concept of an apostle presupposes personal authorization by the holder of the authority, by which above all one becomes an apostle.

68. So also K. Holl, "Der Kirchenbegriff des Paulus in seinem Verhältnis zu dem der Urgemeinde" in *Gesammelte Aufsätze zur Kirchengeschichte, II: Der Osten* (Tübingen, 1928), p. 51.

69. In striking manner in the whole of the New Testament the Lord's brother James, who likewise had an encounter with the Risen One (1 Cor. 15:7) and enjoyed apostolic regard within the circle of the first congregation, is never expressly designated as an apostle, though this does not prove that he was not an apostle. See here my investigation in TD, I, 431.

70. Gal. 1:16a: ἵνα εὐαγγελίζωμαι αὐτὸν (that is, Jesus) ἐν τοῖς ἔθνεσιν.

71. Gal. 1:16b: ε ὐ θ έ ω ς οὐ προσανεθέμην σαρκὶ καὶ αἵματι, οὐδὲ ἀνῆλθον εἰς Ἱεροσόλυμα . . . , ἀλλὰ απῆλθον εἰς Ἀραβίαν.

72. The εὐθέως of Gal. 1:16b in its completely obvious meaning forbids us to accept a development in Paul's consciousness of office in the course of which the extension of his mission to the whole non-Jewish world gradually developed. See also K. Holl, *Der Kirchenbegriff des Paulus,* etc., p. 52, note 3.

73. For the history of these attempts see O. Kietzig, "Die Bekehrung des Paulus" in *Untersuchungen zum Neuen Testament,* ed. H. Windisch, No. 22 (Leipzig, 1932), pp. 55 ff.

74. See pp. 30 f.

75. It would be possible to insert here a sharp criticism of the way the pastoral office has gone in Germany, at least in recent years, insofar as a real consciousness of office is concerned. But today we no longer need the continuous criticism of the past and of the mistakes that have been made, but we need the building up of the new, by which whatever was false will be *practically* overcome. Therefore, with the exception of a short allusion, a detailed criticism is deliberately not taken up.

76. On Gal. 1:6 see note 54 above.

77. See pp. 97 ff.

78. Here one may recall the passages in which he speaks of the coming judgment with an eye to his congregations and his work, but also the formula ἐνώπιον τοῦ θεοῦ, which likewise presupposes the thought of responsibility (cf., for example, 2 Cor. 4:2).

79. See p. 31.

80. K. Holl, "Der ursprüngliche Sinn des Namens Märtyrer," in *Gesammelte Aufsätze,* etc., II, 105, note 1, sees "a puzzle because the apostles did not receive their name from activity directed to the congregation." The name apostle was indispensable because it was necessary to express what Jesus does through the one commissioned by Him, but not what men achieve for Him.

81. For Paul see Acts 9:17 ff. Basically the same thing is to be assumed for Barnabas.

82. For the apostolate of Barnabas see also p. 38 and note 57.

83. See also pp. 38. f.

84. See pp. 36 f.

85. The passages from Acts besides Gal. 2:1 must suffice because Paul hardly comes to speak about such experiences in his own epistles. That he had them is proved, for example, by 2 Cor. 12:1 ff.; that he lived by them is proved by 1 Cor. 4:19 with its subordination of the plans of the apostle under the will of the κύριος.

86. See pp. 16 f. The struggle with the state of emergency regarding the office becomes in part nothing short of a "struggle with the office" even if it takes place today in quite a different manner from that described by A. Pauli, *Im Kampf mit dem Amt* (Munich, 1911).

87. The significance of the Spirit for a consciousness of a sense of mission, as is here being attempted to set it forth, gains special vividness against the background of the claim on the basis of which the representatives of the diatribe of the Cynics and Stoics came to the fore. In this case it never came to a transfer of self-consciousness to a real consciousness of mission and at the same time a conquest of the tension between the commission and the person of the one commissioned (cf. my investigation in TD, I, 411—12). But it could not come to this because one important factor was missing here which, coming authoritatively from outside, would have been capable of producing the necessary close ties between the consciousness and life of the officeholder. In the sphere of the apostolate this important factor was given in the Spirit of Jesus. One will therefore be compelled to say that it was of decisive significance for the apostle's victory over the teachers of the Stoa.

88. On this see pp. 71 ff.
89. Table Talk No. 5189 (WA TR, V, 2).
90. See especially the comments in the *Lectures on Galatians* on 1:1 in *Luther's Works,* American Edition, 26, pp. 15 ff.
91. *Luther's Works,* 26, pp. 16 and 17.
92. Ibid., p. 16.
93. Through the government of the place concerned. Luther accordingly speaks here of the conduct of the *rite vocatus* according to his office.
94. Ibid., p. 18.
95. See here my discussions in TD, I, 430 ff., and p. 34.
96. See K. Deissner, "Das Sendungsbewusstsein der Urchristenheit," *Zeitschrift für systematische Theologie,* 7 (Gütersloh, 1930), 776.
97. Ibid., pp. 776 ff.
98. See pp. 40 f.
99. In our context it is immaterial whether the word was spoken by Jesus or is to be regarded as the creation of the first congregation.
100. Concerning the relationships between John 21:15 ff. and the apostolate see my investigation in TD, I, 434.
101. "Present time" means the whole period between the resurrection and the return of Jesus. This is to be noted also in what follows.
102. Insofar as the Risen One is the Coming One and the future as His future will bring His work to completion, the work by which His congregation already lives.
103. Instead of many examples, cf. for this statement only 1 Peter 5:2 ff. and especially the form ἀρχιποίμην in v. 4, which gives expression to the thought that Jesus is both He who demands an account from the individual ποιμένες as well as and especially the real ποιμήν.
104. A. V. Harless, *Etliche Gewissensfragen hinsichtlich der Lehre von Kirche, Kirchenamt und Kirchenregiment* (Stuttgart, 1862), p. 27.
105. A. F. C. Vilmar, *Die Lehre vom geistlichen Amt* (Marburg, 1870).
106. Ibid., p. 100.
107. F. Delitzsch, *Vier Bücher von der Kirche* (Dresden, 1847), p. 58.
108. Ibid., p. 48.
109. See p. 36.
110. On the critical questions see J. Behm in TD, I, 724 ff., under γλῶσσα.
111. Overcoming ecclesiastical democracy and ecclesiastical parliamentarianism is therefore more than just a prayer of the hour.

112. This is the point on the basis of which the thesis of K. Holl concerning the primacy of the congregation at Jerusalem and the Twelve within early Christianity, to which even Paul at times stooped ("Der Kirchenbegriff des Paulus, etc.: *Gesammelte Aufsätze zur Kirchengeschichte,* II, 44 ff.), must be rejected unconditionally because the starting point is unapostolic.
113. See pp. 32 f.
114. See note 66 above.
115. Kierkegaard, p. 102.
116. Ibid., p. 102.
117. Because of its graphic expression, Luther's version is given [in the German text] and not an exact rendering of the original.
118. Here cf. my investigation in TD, I, 437 ff.
119. See pp. 48 ff.
120. It was already referred to pp. 40 f.
121. See my investigation in TD, I, 44, and A. Schlatter, *Die Theologie der Apostel,* 2d ed. (Stuttgart, 1922), pp. 261 ff.
122. Kierkegaard, p. 105.
123. 1 Cor. 1:4 ff.
124. A. Schlatter, *Die Geschichte des Christus,* 2d ed. (Stuttgart, 1923), p. 532.
125. John 21:1 ff. Cf. here my investigation in TD, I, 434.
126. Schlatter, p. 532.
127. Cf. E. Hirsch, "Luthers Berufung," in *Deutsche Theologie, Luther Sonderheft* (Stuttgart, 1933), pp. 24 ff.
128. Cf. what has already been said on pp. 48 ff.
129. For details see Hirsch, pp. 29 ff.
130. Ibid., p. 27.
131. Ibid., pp. 29 ff., for details.
132. From Karl Holl's "Luthers Urteile über sich selbst," *Gesammelte Aufsätze zur Kirchengeschichte, I: Luther,* 5th ed. (Tübingen, 1927), pp. 392 ff.
133. *Luther's Works,* American Edition, 34, p. 50.
134. So K. Holl, "Luthers Urteile über sich selbst," ibid., p. 393; cf. also p. 396.
135. *Luther's Works: Table Talk,* 54, pp. 12—13.
136. WA, XXX^{3}, 290; XIX, 261.
137. WA, VII, 311.
138. Hirsch, p. 24.
139. Cf. Holl, "Luther und die Schwärmer," ibid., pp. 432 ff.

140. Cf. the passages in Holl, ibid., p. 392.
141. Cf. note 47 above.
142. Cf. pp. 65 ff.
143. Cf. L. A. Petri, *Zum Bau des Hauses Gottes* (Hannover, 1875), pp. 281 ff.; *Gedanken von und für Ordinanden* (1859), pp. 289 ff.; *Das Standesbewusstsein* (1860).
144. Ibid., pp. 292 ff.
145. Cf. pp. 38 f.
146. Petri, *Zum Bau des Hauses Gottes*, p. 365.
147. Cf. p. 15.